Sent

THE KESWICK
YEAR BOOK **2018**

CHRISTOPHER ASH

RICHARD DANNATT

LOUISE MORSE

CHRISTOPHER CHIA

Sent

Serving God's Mission

ALASDAIR PAINE

RODGERS ATWEBEMBEIRE

JONTY ALLCOCK

First published 2018

British Library Cataloguing-in-Publication Data
A catalogue record for this book is available from the British Library.

ISBN: 978–1–78359–994–3
eBook ISBN: 978–1–78359–995–0

Set in Dante 12.5/16pt
Typeset in Great Britain by CRB Associates, Potterhanworth, Lincolnshire
Printed and bound in Great Britain by Ashford Colour Press Ltd, Gosport,
Hampshire

Contents

Introduction

It was with a certain amount of caution as well as anticipation that we arrived at the theme of 'Sent: Serving God's Mission' for the Keswick Convention 2018, the 143rd year. Please don't misunderstand me. The caution came not because the theme is unimportant. Far from it. Every Christian believes 'mission' is important. And, 'Serving God's Mission' is one of the three big convictions that sum up what Keswick Ministries is about, along with 'Hearing God's Word' and 'Becoming like God's Son'. We looked at those in 2016 and 2017. No, the caution came for two reasons.

First, different people mean different things by 'mission', so there is potential for confusion, disagreement and stereotyping. Second, 'mission' tends to be a 'switch-off' topic for many Christians – maybe because of the potential for confusion, maybe because there's a fear of another guilt-inducing 'do-more-mission' event. Perhaps the theme, along with the title 'Sent', could fuel that.

But alongside that caution was a sense of anticipation. Here was a chance to highlight clearly and positively the true nature of mission and for thousands of people to be renewed, refreshed and then sent by the Lord all over the UK and the world.

Our Convention handbook introduction spelled it out:

> We were not the first to be sent by God. God's mission
> doesn't start with us. It starts with God sending his Son
> to redeem the world and sending his Spirit to give us new
> life. At the heart of our mission is the message of Jesus
> Christ. We're not the good news; it's Jesus who's the good
> news. And we're not the ones who change lives; it's the Spirit
> who opens people's eyes to see the glory of Christ. . . .
> Our hope is that together we'll marvel afresh at Jesus –
> God's rescue mission in human form – and this will
> send us out afresh with glad hearts to make Christ known.

The following chapters provide a great sample of the teaching given at the 2018 Convention.

There are five Bible readings on the theme of sending in John's Gospel by Christopher Ash. Christopher unpacks carefully, faithfully and insightfully the sending of John the Baptist, the sending of the Son by the Father and the sending of the Spirit. In the final Bible reading, he helps us to hear in context the force of Jesus' oft-quoted (and oft-misunderstood) words to his disciples, 'As the Father has sent me, I am sending you' (John 20:21).

There are four sermons that come from the evening celebrations across the three weeks. From week 1, which looked at Isaiah 40 – 55, we have Christopher Chia on 'God's Remedy' (Isaiah 42:1–9) and Alasdair Paine on 'God's Suffering Servant' (Isaiah 52:13 – 53:12). From week 2, which looked at Paul the missionary, we have Rodgers Atwebembeire on 'Contesting' (Acts 17:16–34). From week 3, which looked at Philippians, we have Jonty Allcock on 'Gospel Contentment' (Philippians 4:4–23).

The final two contributions to this book draw on the theme of 'Sent'. Richard Dannatt, former head of the British Army, spoke movingly and cogently in the Keswick Lecture in week 1 on 'Sent to the Front Line: Leadership in a Complex World'. Louise Morse gave a seminar on 'Empowering and Engaging Our Seniors', part of a series on being 'Sent Home'.

These contributions give a window into the seminars, Bible readings, evening celebrations and lectures. They provide a snapshot of the engaging, dynamic teaching rooted in the Word of God that saw more than 12,000 people fed, refreshed and sent, whether sent back home – think of the man who had the legion of demons in Mark 5 – or to the ends of the earth.

Alongside this Year Book, we would like to recommend to you two particular books that we produced for 2018. Both are written by Tim Chester, who recently became Chairman of Keswick Ministries. There is the second

edition of *Mission Matters*, a fresh and insightful introduction to mission in our Foundations series. The other
book, *Sent*, is a Bible study resource for groups or individuals on the theme of the Convention.

The Lord alone knows the impact that the 2018 Convention will have. But we can be confident that, when God's
Word is spoken, by the power of his Spirit, lives are
changed. Many will have gone from Keswick all over the
country and all over the world, sent by him to be his
ambassadors.

As you read this book, it is our prayer that you will have
a fresh vision of the sending God, and as you do, so you
too will be inspired and encouraged to serve God's mission,
wherever he sends you!

James Robson
Ministry Director, Keswick Ministries

The Bible Readings

Sent by the Father and the Son
Mission in John's Gospel

Christopher Ash

Christopher Ash first put his trust in Christ as a teenager. He is Writer-in-Residence at Tyndale House, Cambridge. Following thirteen years in secular work, he has been a local church pastor and Director of the Cornhill Training Course. He is married to Carolyn and they have three sons and a daughter. He is currently working on books on the Psalms and John's Gospel.

The Prophet: sent to bear witness to the Son (John 1:1–34)

I am moved again and again by the words of that great old missionary hymn, 'Facing a Task Unfinished':

> with none to heed their crying
> for life and love and light,
> unnumbered souls are dying,
> and pass into the night.[1]

John begins his Gospel on that theme (1:1–5). God has spoken a Word, a divine Word who is fully God with God, in the beginning with no beginning, eternal, the agent of creation through whom all things were made, the only one in whom is life and light and love. This light shines in the darkness. Without this light there is only darkness and death. All is cold, lonely, guilty, and devoid of any sure hope for the future.

Many of you have sat with a loved one as they die. As he or she breathes their final breath and we say that they 'passed on', or 'passed', we cannot help asking: passed where? Passed into the night? Our Bible readings this week engage with this supremely important theme – of life, and love, and light. Of eternal destiny. The theme of the Convention is 'Sent'. And I have chosen to focus on the theme of 'Sent' in John's Gospel. For into that lost world, God sends. There is a lot of sending language in John's Gospel. Sending words appear in John more than in any other Gospel, three times as often as in all of Paul's letters. Nearly a third of all the sending language in the New Testament appears in John's Gospel.

And yet usually, when we hear about mission, the only look-in that John's Gospel gets is John 20:21: 'As the Father has sent me, I am sending you.' That gets quoted a lot. But it's a difficult saying. The Father sent Jesus to work miracles; so does this mean we should be working miracles? The Father sent Jesus to heal and care for the needy; does this mean we should be healing and caring for the needy, that this is the mission of the church? The Father sent Jesus to walk on water; does this mean we should be walking on water? That little saying – 'As the Father sent me, I am sending you' – can become a peg on which to hang all sorts of ideas about Christian mission.

So what I want to do is not to start at the end, where Jesus sends the apostles and then the apostolic church, but to start at the beginning, and to look carefully at the sendings that come before this final sending. Our aim is to grasp the purposes and heart of God who sends; for if we see whom he sends, why he sends, and to what end he sends, we will be given a window into the heart of God. The first sending is a man, John the Baptist. The last sending is of men and women. In between are the most extraordinary sendings of all, in which God the Father sends God the Son, and God the Father and God the Son send God the Holy Spirit. If we can understand something of these sendings, we shall feel the heartbeat of God and know better what Jesus means when he says to each of us, 'As the Father sent me, I am sending you.' And then, I trust and pray, we will leave this Convention and go where Jesus sends, to do what Jesus sends us to do.

A man sent by God

So we begin today with the first sending in John's Gospel: 'There was a man sent from God whose name was John.' John the Baptist, that is, not John the Gospel-writer. Three times we are told he is 'sent' by God (John 1:6, 33; 3:28). Our task this morning is to feel the beating heart of John the Baptist; for if we feel his beating heart we have a window into the deep desires of the God who sent him.

But John 1:6 is a strange verse, do you not think? After the cosmic grandeur of verses 1–5 suddenly, out of nowhere, we meet this man, who isn't even the main focus of the story. We expect to meet the One who is the Word. Instead, we meet a man called John. Before we listen to what John the Baptist says, I want us to take a step back and consider his greatness; for only when we feel his greatness will we listen with real attention to what he says. Here are ten markers of his greatness:

1. The greatness of his birth
He is great because of the account of his birth (Luke 1). It's a tremendous build-up with angels, miracles and a Holy Spirit-inspired song. This boy will be quite somebody!

2. The greatness of his gospel prominence
He is great because of his prominence in all four Gospels at the start of the public ministry of Jesus. He's mentioned in Matthew 3, Mark 1 and Luke 3. In John's Gospel he is centre stage for most of the first chapter. He reappears in chapters 3:22–30 and 5:33–35 and gets a very significant mention at the end of chapter 10 (10:40–42).

3. The greatness of his religious revival
Crowds from Jerusalem and all the region of Judea and Transjordan flocked to hear him and many to be baptized by him (Matthew 3:5). It was a huge revival, way above the evangelical awakening in the eighteenth century, somewhere right up at the top of the Richter scale of religious earthquakes. They say that in late nineteenth-century England a visitor wanted above all else to do two things: to see Queen Victoria and to hear Spurgeon preach. If you visited Judea around AD 30 the question would be: did you hear John the Baptist?

4. The greatness of the variety of those affected by his ministry

The crowds who gathered included the top people in society – the Pharisees, Sadducees and priests from Jerusalem – and the dregs of society – the prostitutes and despised quisling tax-collectors. Everybody from Roman soldiers to prostitutes and priests was there.

5. The greatness of his long-lasting influence

When Herod hears the reports about Jesus, after he has executed John, he thinks Jesus must be John the Baptist, come back from the dead (Matthew 14:2). When Jesus asks his followers who people say he is, one of the most popular answers was: 'Some say John the Baptist' (Mark 8:28). Well after John's death, when Jesus asks the chief priests and elders, 'Was the baptism of John from heaven or from men?' (NASB) they are frightened to say anything against John the Baptist, because of his lasting reputation with the people (Matthew 21:26). Decades later, many years after his death, more than 1,100 miles away by land, in Ephesus, Paul meets a group of disciples of John the Baptist (Acts 19:1–7).

6. The greatness of the expectations he aroused

The people were full of excited expectation, wondering if he might be the Messiah (Luke 3:15).

7. The greatness of what Jesus says about him

Perhaps supremely, he is great because of what Jesus says about him. In John 5:33–35 Jesus calls him 'a lamp that burned and gave light' as he 'testified to the truth'. In Matthew 11:11 Jesus says: 'Truly, I say to you, among those born of women there has not risen anyone greater than John the Baptist' (see also Luke 7:28).

8. The greatness of his pointing away from himself

In John 3:22–30 we read the only Gospel evidence that the ministries of John the Baptist and Jesus overlapped. The disciples of Jesus were baptizing as people came into their group; and John the Baptist is still baptizing. The scope for rivalry must have been intense. And, sure enough, people come to John the Baptist and say, 'look, he is baptizing, and everyone is going to him' (3:26). I would have hated that. I want to be the success, the focus of people's attention and admiration. It's a little like when you leave a job. There is something ugly in us that would feel just a little pleased to hear that our successors are not doing so well. If our successors do better than us it's hard to take. But what does John the Baptist say? 'Good! You follow them. That is why I came, to do myself out of a job.' He describes himself like the best man at a wedding. I remember a season in life when I was unmarried and kept being best man for friend after friend, or so it seemed. It was a privilege. But there was something in my heart that would have preferred to be the bridegroom! Yet here is perhaps the greatest religious leader the world had known who loves to sing the praises of the Bridegroom and to rejoice as he woos and weds his bride. It is a mark of the greatness of John the Baptist, the man sent

by God, that he gladly, joyfully, pointed away from himself
(verse 30).

9. The greatness of his vindicated testimony

Near the end of his public ministry, Jesus crossed the
Jordan 'to the place where John had been baptizing in
the early days . . . many people came to him. They said,
"Though John never performed a sign [this great religious
leader never did a miracle, never performed a healing],
all that John said about this man was true"' (John
10:40–41).

What a wonderful epitaph. How wonderful if they
were to put on your gravestone or mine, 'This man, this
woman, never did any miracles, but they spoke about
Jesus Christ. And everything they said about Jesus was
true.'

10. He is great because of what he says about Jesus

The reason John the Baptist is so overwhelmingly great
is that he is the final and concluding voice of centuries of
Old Testament witness. 'The Law and the Prophets were
proclaimed until John' says Jesus (Luke 16:16). When
we listen to John the Baptist we do not hear the random
thoughts of a religious eccentric; this is the summing
up of the testimony of all the prophets from Moses
onwards, the closing speech from the Old Testament
witness box.

He is a very great man. So let us listen to him.

What John says about Jesus

In John 1:6–34 we hear the testimony of this very great man to Jesus Christ. I want us to notice the nature of his task, the reason for his task, the grandeur of his task, the drama of his task, and – as our main emphasis – the focus of his task.

1. The nature of his task: to bear witness to Jesus Christ

'He came as a *witness*, to *testify* concerning that light . . . He himself was not the light; he came only as a *witness* to the light' (verses 7–8). Again and again we are told that John the Baptist's task was to bear witness to Jesus (see John 1:15, 19, 32; 3:26; 5:33).

2. The reason for his task: that all people may believe

His purpose is that all sorts of people, from all over the world and all down the centuries, might believe in the light, might find life (verse 7). His purpose is precisely the purpose of the whole Old Testament, that through the Old Testament Scriptures you and I can become wise for salvation through faith in Jesus Christ (2 Timothy 3:15).

3. The grandeur of his task: the divine-human person of Jesus Christ

In verses 9–18 we learn that the one to whom John bears witness is astonishingly, wonderfully, uniquely, supremely great. 'The true light that gives light to everyone was coming into the world' (verse 9). It is not that everyone sees it, but that there is no other light that can be seen. And this eternal Word who was with God and was God became flesh, became a man (verse 14). Without for a moment losing his nature as God, he took upon himself our human nature. His human nature and his divine nature were united in one indivisible person, without either nature being compromised or mixed up into some third composite nature, so that in his perfect humanity he never ceased to be God, and in his perfect deity he became forever human. This incarnation is the greatest miracle in the universe.

What was foreshadowed in the Old Testament taber-nacle was fulfilled in him; God dwelling with men and women. And in him is the fulfilment of all the covenant promises. Verse 16, 'Out of his fullness', the fullness of God incarnate, 'we have all received grace in place of grace already given', grace upon grace, new covenant grace upon old covenant grace. The law (covenant grace in anticipation) was given through Moses, and it was a good, grace-filled, wonderful, spiritual law; but grace and truth – covenant fulfilment – came through Jesus Christ. And so he names Jesus Christ for the first time, with awe and wonder in his voice (verse 17).

Now the Son makes visible the invisible Father; he publishes him, exegetes him. Because the Son dwells from all eternity in the most intimate closeness with the Father, he, and he alone, can make him known (verse 19). This is more than informational access; this is relational. The Son dwells by the Spirit with the Father in a fellowship of infinite intimacy and perfect love. The Father loves the Son

(John 3:35); he has loved him from before the foundation of the world (John 17:24). When Jesus publishes the Father to a watching world, he placards before the world the overflow of eternal love.

All this sums up the testimony of John the Baptist, which is the testimony of the Old Testament. This is the grandeur of his witness: the subject is the one through whom the world was made, the one who is and was eternally God with God, who became flesh and dwelt among us, in whom all the promises of the Old Testament, or old covenant, find their fulfilment.

And now, in verses 19–28, we begin to sense the drama, the rising tension, of his task.

4. *The drama of his task*

The John the Baptist phenomenon is so big that an official delegation is sent from the temple staff – priests and Levites – to ask him, 'Who are you?' First, because of the speculation, he volunteers, 'I am not the Messiah' (verse 20). We know from Luke 3:15 that 'the people were waiting expectantly and were all wondering in their hearts if John might possibly be the Messiah.' John denied it here and again in chapter 3:28.

He also denied he was Elijah, the great prophet who would be sent by God before the great and terrible day of the Lord (Malachi 4:5). He preached judgment and repentance as Elijah did, and the angel told his father he would 'go on before the Lord, in the spirit and power of Elijah . . .' (Luke 1:17). Jesus himself said that, 'If you are willing to accept it, he is the Elijah who was to come' (Matthew 11:14; see also Matthew 17:10–13). So, in one sense, John is an Elijah-kind-of-figure. But not the literal Elijah, come back from heaven.

The delegation then ask John, 'Are you the Prophet?' In Deuteronomy 18:15–22 Moses says that the Lord will send 'a prophet like me' to replace him after he dies. There had been plenty of prophets who spoke the truth like Moses but no prophet who redeemed a people out of slavery like Moses. 'Are you *the* Prophet?' means 'Are you this final Prophet who will not only speak the Word of God but redeem the people out of slavery?' 'No,' says John. There may even be a hint of frustration in his shortening answers. He really doesn't want to talk about himself. 'You are asking the wrong question when you ask me, "Who are *you*?" The question I have come to answer is, "Who is *he*?"'

If John the Baptist insisted he was not the one to offer a changed life, then the best and most truthful thing that liberal humanism, militant atheism, Hinduism, Buddhism, Islam, or just a general cobbled together philosophy of English niceness can say is, 'No, I am not what you need. If you follow me, you will be forever dissatisfied. At some point you will hit the buffers and know in your heart that you cannot find in me the one you most deeply need.'

The priests and Levites finally say, verse 22, 'Give us an answer to take back to those who sent us. What do you say about yourself?' John replies, 'I am the voice of one calling in the wilderness, "Make straight [prepare] the way for the Lord."' Then the delegation moves from questions of identity to the question of authority; from 'Who are you?' to 'Why do you baptize?' They go on to ask him why he baptizes, if he is just a voice, for baptism initiates people into something; you can't start baptizing people without authority. John's answer was effectively, 'I do not baptize to initiate people into something; I baptize to prepare them for someone. One so much greater that my ministry – for all its scope, influence and reputation – will fade into obscurity by comparison with him.'

We know that John the Baptist was the supporting act, the warm-up act. But his effect was so big, so influential, and so dramatic, that people must have wondered what the main act could possibly be. And so the tension rises.

5. The focus of his task

And so, finally, in verses 29–34, we reach the climax of John's testimony. There are, I think, five pointers that sum up the testimony of John the Baptist, five things that John testifies about Jesus:

a. His relation to sin

'The next day John saw Jesus coming towards him.' It was an electric moment: 'Behold!' or 'Look! Look! LOOK! The Lamb of God, who takes away the sin of the world!' (verse 29). The Lamb – perhaps the Passover Lamb, but certainly a sacrificial Lamb provided by God the Father – who dies as a substitute sacrifice to take away the sin of the world. The animal sacrifices were a foreshadowing, a promise, an anticipation that one day there will be a true sacrifice for sins. And now into that sin-spoiled world here comes the sin-bearer, the Lamb of God.

b. His relation to time

Verse 30, 'This is the one I meant when I said, "A man who comes after me has surpassed me because he was before me."' This sin-bearing Lamb is not simply a man who reached great heights of religious attainment. No, he is God with God from all eternity; he was 'before me'; he is God made flesh.

c. His relation to repentance

John says, verse 31, 'I myself did not know him.' John was Jesus' cousin, and he certainly knew him in that human sense (Luke 1:36 tells us that Mary and Elizabeth were relatives); in Matthew 3:13–14 he tries to dissuade him from being baptized. But he did not know Jesus in the sense of recognizing him in his full identity as the incarnate Word, not until he saw the Spirit come down on him at his baptism. That was an eye-opening moment for John the Baptist.

And there is something about John's baptism ministry that means Jesus is revealed to Israel (verse 31). In Luke 7:29–30 we read that the people who had been baptized by John responded rightly to Jesus, whereas the people who refused John's baptism refused Jesus. He is revealed to those in Israel who submit to John the Baptist's baptism, to those into whose hearts God puts repentance. Those who submit to John's baptism submit to Jesus and find in him the forgiveness of sins. There is an indissoluble connection between Jesus and repentance from sins.

d. His relation to the Spirit and the human heart

Verse 32, 'I saw the Spirit come down from heaven as a dove' – in some strange way the invisible Spirit of God became for a time visible – 'and remain on him.' In the old covenant period the Spirit came upon prophets so they prophesied; he came upon some of the judges so they could lead; he came upon some kings. But he did not 'remain'. But John emphasizes that, on this man, the Spirit comes to remain, to abide, to indwell fully and for ever.

And therefore this man, uniquely in human history, is the man of the Spirit. He is 'the one who will baptize with the Holy Spirit', who has the astonishing authority to pour the personal presence of God into the depths of a human heart to change a man or woman for ever (verse 22). The prophets prophesied that one day God would pour out his Spirit on every one of his people (Joel 2:28) and turn their hearts of stone into hearts of flesh (Ezekiel 36:26). How the believers longed for that day. And now, here he is!

e. His relation to the Father

John says, verse 34, 'I have seen and I testify that this is God's Chosen One' (or perhaps 'God's Son'). This man uniquely is in intimate and eternal relationship with God the Father. He and he alone can make the Father known (1:18).

In summary, in relation to God this man is the chosen one, the unique Son of the Father, the man of the Spirit, in eternal intimacy with the Father by the Spirit. And in relation to men and women, this man is the sin-bearer and therefore the giver of the Holy Spirit to men and women. This man does in reality what in the old covenant is seen in foreshadowing and prophecy.

Three major directions of response

As we reflect on this testimony we learn:

1. *How to read the Old Testament*
   The burden and purpose of the Old Testament is the burden and purpose of John the Baptist. It is a voice bearing testimony to Jesus. It is the testimony of the Father, by the Spirit, to the Son. We learn that the purpose of the Old Testament is to lead us to faith in Jesus Christ (see 2 Timothy 2:15). And we learn to put our Old Testament spectacles on as we read John's Gospel.
2. *The importance of grasping – as much as we can – the divine-human person of Jesus Christ, the second person of the Trinity*
   The five foci of John's testimony (Jesus' relation to sin, time, the Father, repentance, and the Spirit) point in two directions. They point towards the identity of Jesus in relation to the Father and the Spirit, the one in intimate relationship with the Father by the Spirit, the one outside and beyond of time, the one with the fullness of deity dwelling

within him. We hear the testimony of John the
Baptist to the divine-human person of Jesus Christ
and we too are filled with awe.

3. *The centrality of the forgiveness of sins and the baptism*
   of the Holy Spirit in the Father's testimony to the Son
   When God the Father sends John the Baptist he
   does so to bear testimony to his Son as the sin-bearer
   and the giver of the Holy Spirit. We need to feel the
   burden of our sins if we are to wonder with John
   at the appearance of the sin-bearer. Christianity
   is a rescue religion. It is not a lifestyle choice,
   a philosophy to make you feel better about yourself,
   or guidance for how to live well; it is a message of
   taken-away sins for burdened sinners. Too often,
   it seems to me, when speaking of Jesus we say things
   like, 'Jesus gives me purpose in life' or 'Jesus has
   given me peace of mind and heart.' Well, he may
   have done, and we should thank him when he does.
   But Christianity says something much deeper:
   Behold, the Lamb of God who takes away sins!

   Furthermore, it is a message of transformation as
   the Holy Spirit of God comes to dwell in the human
   heart and spirit, to change the human heart by
   working in us at the very deepest level of human
   personhood. John says: 'I can baptize you with water;
   I can get you wet on the outside. But this man can
   change you on the inside because he is the man
   of the Spirit.' What the prophets spoke of, as they
   looked forward to the new covenant, he will bring

to pass. When Joel and Ezekiel spoke of the Spirit of God in the heart, this he will fulfil.

Conclusion

So let us heed the testimony of this man sent by God. The heart of the Father is that we learn that the Son dwells from all eternity in the bosom of the Father, in that fellowship of infinite love by the Spirit. The heart of the Father is that we feel the wonder that this man, this incarnate Word, is the sin-bearer and the giver of the Holy Spirit, and that, if we repent and are baptized and come to him in faith, we too will receive the forgiveness of our sins and the gift of the Holy Spirit.

A man sent by God – because,

> with none to heed their crying
> for life, and love, and light,
> unnumbered souls are dying
> and pass into the night.

And John the Baptist is sent to cry, 'Look! Look! LOOK! The Lamb of God, the man of the Spirit who gives the Spirit, the one and only Son of the Father. Look! And live!'

Note

1. Frank Houghton, 'Facing a Task Unfinished', 1931.

The Son: sent to give life by his death (John 6:1–59)

We come this morning to one of the most extraordinary chapters in the Gospels. At the start, after the feeding of the 5,000, the people want to acclaim Jesus as King; by the end they have almost all abandoned him. In verse 67 Jesus has to ask the Twelve if they too want to leave. From fame to desolation – it is an extraordinary transition. How come Jesus could be so astonishingly popular and then – in almost the twinkling of an eye – so alone? If we can grasp what causes this change, what it is about the mission of Jesus that causes such a scandal, we will be close to the core of the heart of God the Father.

We considered yesterday John the Baptist, 'a man sent by God'. We considered how, when one sends another and the other goes willingly, the will and heartbeat of the sent one reveals to us something of the will and heartbeat of the one who sends. This morning we come to a sending that perfectly, fully, wonderfully, flawlessly, reveals the heartbeat of the Father who sends. We come, that is, to the sending of the Son.

Since the 1950s it has been a commonplace in mission studies to say that mission is rooted in the so-called *Missio Dei*, and most significantly in the sending by the Father of the Son. But, rather like John 20:21, the phrase *Missio Dei* has become what one writer calls 'a shopping cart' into which people could put whatever they thought mission should be. Subjects as diverse as gender equality, racial reconciliation, creation care, inter-religious dialogue, and the transformation of society have all been included as part of the *Missio Dei*.

So I want us to see what we can learn from John 6 about the heartbeat of the Father who sent the Son, and the heartbeat of the Son who is sent. I think we shall learn something of enduring importance about why the mission of the church, the true *Missio Dei*, will always be counter-cultural and unpopular, and always tending to segue into something more acceptable.

When we come to chapter 6, we watch the fourth of John's seven signs, the only miracle recorded in all four Gospels. Jesus is in Galilee, in the north, the place where there isn't really hostility. Indeed, there is some kind of popularity. In verses 1–24 we have the historical description of the sign. Then from verse 25 to the end of the chapter we have sustained teaching.

Jesus is sent as food for a greater journey

I want us to walk through verses 1–24 first superficially and then deeply. Here's the superficial walk:

> After this Jesus crossed over to the other side of the Sea
> of Galilee. That's just how it was. And a large crowd just
> happened to follow him, because they were fascinated
> by his healing miracles. Over on the other side, Jesus
> happened to go up a hill and they all sat down. It happened
> to be Passover, spring-time. They weren't near markets,
> so there was a discussion about how to get food. Jesus took
> a small picnic, multiplied it and fed them all. They gathered
> up the overflow into some baskets. After this, the people
> said, 'Wow!' and wanted to make Jesus their king. But
> Jesus slipped away and – by walking on water – helped his
> followers get back to the Jewish side of the lake. The crowd
> followed the next day and were very intrigued and amazed.
> Then Jesus says to them, verse 26, 'I tell you the truth, you
> are looking for me, not because you saw miraculous signs
> but because you ate the loaves and had your fill.'

They thought eating the loaves *was* the sign. But Jesus said they ate the loaves but didn't see the sign. In one sense, of course they saw the signs; that is precisely why they are there, because they saw the healing signs and now also the feeding sign. But, no, says Jesus, you didn't really *see* the sign. Now let's look more closely at the story and see what's really going on.

We join a leader away from the Promised Land, the other side of a sea. A large crowd is with him. The leader goes up a mountain to teach them and again up a mountain later to be by himself. It is the time of the Passover, with all that is remembered then. These people are in the wilderness where there is no food. Miraculously, they are fed in the wilderness. The leftovers are put in twelve baskets. They say the leader must be the prophet like Moses. And then the leader takes some of them miraculously across water and into the Promised Land.

Does that ring any bells? Of course! You know the story of a multitude crossing a sea, travelling through the wilderness to a mountain, how their leader asks God, 'Where can I get meat for all these people?' (Numbers 11:13), how he feeds them, how the number twelve speaks of the twelve tribes of that people, and so on. To those who know their Old Testament, as these people did, there are deafening echoes reverberating around of an earlier story, the defining story of Israel and Moses.

That journey echoed through the Old Testament in different ways (see 2 Kings 4:42–44; Ruth 2:14). And yet there has been no prophet quite like Moses. True prophets spoke the truth like Moses, and John the Baptist was the greatest. But no prophet has taken the people of God out of slavery and into the Promised Land since Moses (Deuteronomy 34:10–12). And at one level they get the echoes of the earlier story. In verse 14 we read, 'the people saw the miraculous sign' – that's why they say he must be the prophet like Moses, who did signs and wonders, who showed mighty power when he led a large multitude, at the time of the Passover, out of Egypt, across a sea, and fed them in the wilderness, taking them to a mountain, to Mount Sinai.

And yet Jesus says they didn't see the signs. They saw and enjoyed loaves of bread (verse 26). What they didn't see is where the signposts point. This is not a re-run of the story of food for the physical journey of the Hebrews – out of slavery in Egypt, through the Red Sea, across the wilderness, to Mount Sinai, and then on to the Promised Land. No! This is about a greater journey.

Verse 27, 'Do not work for food that spoils [perishes], but for food that endures to eternal life [the life of the age to come], which the Son of Man will give you. For on him God the Father has placed his seal of approval [that is, the Holy Spirit].' Jesus says, 'Do not work for food that spoils.' I want to pause to reflect on this before we go any further. We are creatures of desire. We have appetites, hungers, thirsts, wants, needs. Our lives are shaped and driven by our desires, perhaps a desire to be loved and appreciated, a longing to be safe, a yearning for success, a wanting for intimacy or for happy and satisfying family relationships, the painful longing for conception and birth of a child, a hope for deep friendships, a desire to be beautiful or healthy or comfortable. Appetites are all around us and deep within us. The Buddhist ideal of Nirvana as the absence of desire, transcending desire, really won't wash. Loss of appetite is a well-known symptom of depression. Desire, or appetite, is what gets us out of bed in the morning; it is what makes us tick. So it is important to think about our appetites.

It is not wrong to want food and drink to stay alive; it is not wrong to want to keep healthy; it is not wrong to desire a sound mind or health of spirits; it is not wrong to long for healthy relationships, for reconciliation where there is alienation, for good friendships, for intimacy in marriage; it is not wrong to want satisfaction in our work, a measure of success and fulfilment. For sure, these hungers get disordered and distorted. A hunger for food can become gluttony. An enjoyment of a glass of wine can become alcoholism. A hope for fulfilment can become an idolatry of success. A yearning for intimacy can become a sinful lust. And so on. But at root these are natural desires.

And yet there is an insatiability about them. Jesus calls them 'food that spoils'. He gives one reason not to prioritize or set our hopes on what satisfies our natural appetites: whatever fills our hunger in this age always spoils, never lasts. Think about it: you are filled by a good meal, and tomorrow you want another one; you are healed of an illness today, and next year you need healing from another one; your desire for fulfilment is met by some success this year, but the success fades; you are only as good as your last victory; no-one cares this year that you did well in an exam ten years ago, that you did well in a job ten years ago, that you were happy in marriage ten years ago. Jesus comes as nourishment for a deeper journey, a journey that the exodus travels only foreshadowed. He calls himself 'food that endures' – food that lasts, keeps going and keeps us going – 'to eternal life', the life of the age to come.

So what does it mean to really see the signs? It means to read the story at a deeper level. It means to grasp that the healings are not about healing and the feeding is not about feeding, in this age. This is not saying that Jesus is the leader who will satisfy our natural appetites. This is not the health, wealth and prosperity gospel; this is not the therapeutic gospel, to make me feel better about myself. This is not the gospel that says that Jesus is sufficient for all my desires in this life. Jesus is not the one who gives me a meal, only for me to be hungry again; he is not the one to make me healthy, only for me to get sick again; not the one to give me success, only to leave me hungry for more success; not the one to give me love, only to see that love grow cold or sour or end in bereavement; not the one to feed me with food that spoils.

Oh, in the kindness and common grace of God, he does give us many good things in this age. He gives us food and drink, clothing, shelter, friendships, happy marriages, harmonious family relationships, a measure of success and fulfilment. He does give us some of these things some of the time. But this is not the purpose for which Jesus was sent.

So what does it mean? It means we are a people on a journey, walking through a wilderness world in which our appetite for God cannot be met by the world through which we walk; and yet it means we are a people heading for the Promised Land, for the new heavens and new earth, the new creation, the life of the age to come. We feel the misery of the wilderness, the hunger and the fear. We are a people with a past, a present and a future. A past in which we have been redeemed from slavery to sin; a present in which our leader sustains us through the wilderness; a future in which all our deepest longings for God will be fulfilled. We are a people on a journey to the age to come. We do not belong to this age. To see the sign, to grasp where the signpost points, is to understand that this is our identity. In an age dominated by appetites, it is to be set free from having our lives defined by those appetites.

Jesus is sent as food from a higher source and for a precious people

Next, I want to take verses 28–51 and see in it two big strands: Jesus is sent as food from a higher source and food for a precious people. Sometimes, especially in John, instead of getting points sequentially, we seem to get them woven together like a multi-coloured thread. The first strand I want to focus on is the identity of Jesus Christ: who is he and from whence did he come? Because Jesus nourishes for a greater journey, he needs to come from a higher source.

John the Baptist was 'sent from God'. All the prophets were sent from God, so what is the difference with Jesus being 'sent from God'? How does Jesus differ from a prophet? Of course, that is an important question in mission to Muslims, for the Qur'an acknowledges that

Jesus is a prophet, and mission to Jehovah's Witnesses, and indeed to any who deny the full divine nature of Jesus Christ. I think we need to give closer attention to this than we sometimes do. In this passage Jesus signals some of the ways that his 'sending' is different from the 'sending' of John the Baptist.

1. We must believe in Jesus

In verse 28 they ask, 'What must we do to do the works God requires?' Jesus answers that the 'work' is 'to believe in the one he has sent'. This is what it means to seek the food that endures to eternal life. That expression 'believe in' is never used of the prophets. You were to hear and heed John the Baptist; but not to believe in him. But the one the Father has sent, Jesus the Son, is to be the object of your faith; you are to believe in him.

The people understand that this is a big claim because they refer back to the sign of the manna in the wilderness, which demonstrated the authority of Moses, and they ask: 'What sign then will you give that we may see it and believe you?' (verse 30). That is a little ironic, given the astonishing sign they have just witnessed! There is something in un-belief that is always seeking more evidence, when they have plenty. But they understand that Jesus is claiming something bigger than being a prophet.

2. Jesus comes down from heaven

And so Jesus begins to use the second strand of his claim, with the language of coming 'from heaven'. In verse 32 he moves them from the manna of Exodus 16 to the reality that the manna foreshadowed. You think Moses gave you bread from heaven. But what is happening now is different in three ways. It is different in its source, for 'it is *my Father* who gives . . .' It is different in its nature, for this is 'true bread'. In John's Gospel 'true' is not the opposite of 'false'; true is the opposite of provisional. True means solid, substantial, real, final, the reality which the old covenant types foreshadowed – the true vine in chapter 15; the way, the truth and the life in chapter 14, and so on. The manna was not false but it was provisional, a shadow of the reality to come. Different in its source, different in its nature, and different in its tense: Moses gave you manna in the past, but my Father 'gives you the true bread from heaven'. This bread 'comes down from heaven and gives life to the world' (verse 33). You would never say that of a prophet. But here is one who, in his full humanity, may simultaneously be said to have come down from heaven. And he says it again and again (see verse 38, 41, 42, 50, 51, 58).

So his sending is different, because we are to believe in him. It is different because he has come down from heaven. We will see the third reason in a minute. But now the focus switches from the identity of Jesus to the precious people for whom he came. I was sent to give 'life to the world' (verse 33), to men and women by nature hostile to God and unwilling to acknowledge the One through whom they were made.

But to whom exactly will he give life? Verse 35: 'I am the bread of life. Whoever comes to me will never go hungry, and whoever believes in me will never be thirsty.' He gives life to all who will come to him, believe in him. Anyone, every one, young or old, clever or uneducated, rich or poor, slave or free, to each and every one who comes to him in faith, Jesus gives life. No unsatisfied appetite in this life, no unfulfilled longing, no grief, no sadness, can change the fact that, in having Jesus, I have the spiritual nourishment for my soul that will sustain and keep me right the way through to the age to come.

But there is more. Verse 36, 'You have seen me and still you do not believe.' So there is a mystery here which Jesus teaches us about in verses 37–39. In the hidden purposes of God in all eternity, the Father has given to Jesus a people, and every one of those people will come to him. They join his travelling caravan of pilgrim people on their way from slavery to the Promised Land of the new creation. As they travel with him, he will never expel them. Not one of those whom the Father has entrusted to Jesus will be lost by the wayside (verses 38–39).

In the hidden purposes of God, the Father gives particular men and women to Jesus. He says to his Son, 'Will you take this man, this woman, this child? Will you accept them? Will you keep them to the end and raise them up on the last day?' Jesus solemnly promises, 'Yes, Father, I will. I will turn none away. I will keep each to the end. I will do just exactly what you desire, for my will is to do your will; I want what you want; I will raise them up on the last day.' No true sheep of Jesus will be left behind. No matter what trials, sickness or mental illness befalls you, once Jesus has you he will keep you until resurrection morning.

So there is this wonderful hidden purpose of God. Why did you put your trust in Christ? Because you had religious perception and could see that Jesus was true? Possibly. But in eternity, you came to Jesus because the Father gave you to Jesus. Jesus accepted you because the Father entrusted you to Jesus. You hope for final resurrection because the Father gave you to Jesus and Jesus promises to keep you to the end.

And then, in verse 40, the camera angle changes: 'For my Father's will is that everyone who looks to the Son and believes in him shall have eternal life, and I will raise them up at the last day.' The arms of Jesus are open wide. The appeal of the evangelist is to everyone and anyone. You hear the appeal; you respond; you come to Jesus; and then you find that – wonder of wonders – from all eternity the Father entrusted you to Jesus, and that is why you chose to come, and that is why Jesus accepts you and that is why Jesus promises to keep you. The invitation is open and to all; the assurance rests not on your or my decision but on the eternal purpose of God.

Then, in verses 41–42, we switch back to the 'identity of Jesus' strand. They say, 'Is this not Jesus, the son of Joseph, whose father and mother we know? How can he now say, "I came down from heaven"?' And in asking that they ask the most fundamental question about the person of Jesus of Nazareth: how can he be fully and really a man and at the same time fully and really God the Son? This is the big question about Jesus. And the answer is the greatest miracle in the history of the world. John's Gospel looks at the person of Jesus from two directions. First, Jesus is a man uniquely filled with the Holy Spirit (1:32–34; 3:34; 6:27). Second, Jesus is the eternal Son of God (1:1–18; 5:26; 6:33, 38, 50–51). How is this possible? How can both be true? The key statement to unlock this is John 1:14: 'The Word became flesh.'

The eternal Word, God with God, came down from heaven and became flesh, became human. Had he not 'come down', had he been fully God but not fully human, he could not be the bread *come down* from heaven to give life to the world. Had he been fully human but not fully God, he could not be the bread come down *from heaven* to give life to the world. Only the divine-human Jesus can be the Father's gift of bread from heaven to lost sinners. Wonderfully, the second person of the Trinity became flesh, so that in Jesus of Nazareth there is the fullness of the divine nature and a fully authentic human nature, indivisibly in one person. And because he came down from heaven as the Son of God incarnate, he can feed us for the greater journey to the new heavens and new earth.

And now we switch back to the 'precious people' theme. Verse 44: 'No one can come to me unless the Father who sent me draws them [singular – him or her], and I will raise them up at the last day.' The natural human being will never come to Jesus in true faith. But wonderfully the Father does draw people to Jesus. In verse 45 Jesus quotes from a prophecy in Isaiah 54, in which God promises his people that there will be a time in the future when they will be taught by God (Isaiah 54:13). And when they are taught by God then they will come to Jesus (verse 45). It is because the beginning of the Christian life rests on the decision of the Father and the faithfulness of Jesus that its end is guaranteed. And because the end of the journey is guaranteed by the will of the Father and the pledge of the Son, the life of the age to come begins the day we put our trust in Jesus (verse 47).

So here's the difference between the shadow and the reality (48–51). Verse 49, 'Your ancestors ate the manna in the wilderness, yet they died.' They were in the travelling caravan, and they died in the wilderness, a whole generation. How can we know this won't happen to us? Verse 50, 'Here is the bread that comes down from heaven, which anyone may eat and not die.' You eat the manna and you may still die and not reach the Promised Land. But you 'eat' Jesus and you will never die. The generation that ate the manna died in the wilderness because they fixated on the food that perishes. But those who receive the food who is Jesus will never die. This is very emphatic.

So in verses 28–51 we see these two strands: Jesus comes as food from a higher source; and Jesus comes as food for a precious people. These strands are united because God the Father is present in both. Jesus comes from God the Father because God the Father has counted this people precious and entrusted them to Jesus. Our security rests on the love of the Father and the harmony of will between the Father and the Son. It is a wonderful security.

So how come the chapter ends so badly, with mass desertion?

Jesus is sent to die

The theme of verses 28–51a has been Jesus' claim, 'I am the bread of life', the bread given by God, come down from heaven, to give life to the world. But at the end of verse 51 Jesus adds a strange twist: 'This bread is my flesh, which I will give for the life of the world.' Not surprisingly, it provokes a sharp argument and the question: 'How can this man give us his flesh to eat?' Far from backtracking, Jesus makes it worse, verse 53, 'Very truly I tell you, unless you eat the flesh of the Son of Man and drink his blood, you have no life in you.' Not only eating human flesh but drinking human blood! It sounds horrible.

So what does Jesus mean? The first clue is in verse 51: 'which I will *give* for the life of the world'. Jesus' flesh and blood is *given* to be eaten and drunk. The second clue is the words 'flesh' and 'blood'. In a living body, flesh and blood are inseparable: it is death that separates flesh from blood; blood is poured out when a creature dies violently. The word 'blood' in the Old and New Testaments means a life poured out in violent death. To devour someone's flesh or drink their blood means to gain some benefit from their death. When the Hebrews ate the flesh of the Passover lamb and spread its blood on the doorposts, they appropriated for themselves the benefits of a sacrificial death. Jesus is saying that by his sacrificial death, his flesh given for us, his blood poured out for us, he makes it possible for us to enjoy the benefits of that death in our place. He dies my death, that I may be raised on the last day.

In verses 56–57 Jesus teaches that one of the great benefits of his death will be union with him and with the Father. This is union with Christ, being organically joined with Christ, so that when he died, we died, and when he was raised, we were raised. Just as Jesus is in union with the Father, so that his life and the Father's life are inseparably joined, 'so the one who feeds on me will live because of me.' To be joined to Jesus happens only as we appropriate the benefits of his death. Life comes to us only by his death. Jesus is speaking metaphorically, but it is a shocking and striking metaphor. He says that unless I appropriate for myself the benefits of his terrible, violent, sacrificial death for sinners, I have no share in him. But if I do have – as Charles Wesley put it – 'an interest in the Saviour's blood',[1] then I am united with him just as he is united with the Father.

The shock – and it is this that causes so many of his disciples to drift away – is that the food we need is the crucified Jesus. It would be hard to find a more graphic instance in the New Testament where the scandal of the cross is placarded before us more strongly. And yet it is vital. We are on a journey through this age. The 'foods' we find in this age all spoil – whether it be literal food and water, health, intimacy, success, love or beauty. They spoil and there is nothing we can do about that. The question is: where will the journey end? Will we reach the Promised

Land, the new heavens and new earth? For that we need our sins forgiven; we need the food that is the sacrificial substitutionary death of the divine-human person of Jesus. We need food from a higher source. We need the food of his broken body and outpoured blood.

This message will never play well in the world. The world wants a message that is this-world focused, that is intelligible in terms of this world, that does not have at its heart the scandalous declaration that your sin is so terrible that only the broken body and outpoured blood of the incarnate Son of God can atone for it.

And yet this message is the only message that offers men and women the food that endures to eternal life. How vital then that you and I feed on Jesus' death for us; how vital that we acknowledge that without that death we have no life; how vital that we never move beyond the cross; how wonderful to have an interest in his blood. How vital that the message of the cross, the scandal of the cross, be right at the heart of our mission. For this is the heartbeat of the Father who gave a people to Jesus. This is the heartbeat of the Son, who is committed to saving that people, who came to die that he might achieve just what the Father sent him to do.

What is the heart of the heartbeat of God the Father? It is the heartbeat of God the Son, which is that holy determination to die for sinners, that he may take every one of his chosen people on that journey all the way from the slavery, that Egypt foreshadowed under the Pharaohs, to the new heavens and new earth foreshadowed in the

Promised Land. Only he can do this – the one who is fully human and fully God, the one who comes down from heaven and is made flesh for us. It is for this he is sent and for this he comes with a will perfectly aligned with the Father's will.

We will only understand what it is for us to be sent if we grasp the wonder of this sending – the greater journey, the higher source, the chosen people and the violent death. This is mission that keeps a sure focus on the new heavens and new earth; mission that never compromises on the full wonder of the divine-human person of Jesus Christ; mission that holds out to men and women the promise, to all who will trust in Christ, that final resurrection is assured. This is mission with the cross at its heart.

Note

1. Charles Wesley, 'And Can It Be', 1738.

The Son: sent to make the Father known (John 12:37–50)

Preaching during the closing stages of the Second World War, the German pastor and theologian Helmut Thielicke spoke of the happy times in the world as 'like tiny islands in an ocean of blood and tears. The history of the world,' he went on to say, 'is a story of war, deeply marked with the hoofprints of the apocalyptic horsemen. It is the story of humanity without a Father – *so it seems.*'[1]

Our longing for – and the significance of – our human fathers is a pointer to our need for a heavenly Father. The heavenly Father is not a substitute for a human father; nor is he the imaginary projection of our need for a father figure (as Freud would have it). No, it is the other way around: he is the one to whom all our natural longings point. Our longings for a father are the echo of our yearning and deep need for a heavenly Father. He is the satisfaction of our deepest human longings and needs.

Jesus came to make known the Father to men and women in a world of blood and tears. The defining event in the history of the universe was when Jesus of Nazareth made the invisible Father God known. In substance – as we saw yesterday – he does this by his sin-bearing death. But when it comes to our hearing and understanding the Father, he makes the Father known by words. The Father sends Jesus, and Jesus speaks to make the Father known. He is sent to speak words, words that are now written. Jesus is sent to make the Father known; he makes the Father known by written words, by the Bible.

Perhaps you are thinking two things. First, logically, you are asking how we got from the spoken words of Jesus to the written words of the Bible. That's a very fair question and we will come to that. But also – I guess – you are feeling uneasy about focusing on a book because books are dead. And what is true for books in general is surely also true for the Bible. I have on my shelf many Bibles and not one of them has put a hand on my shoulder, talked to me and said, 'Let me make the Father known to you.' Even my King James version has not done that! Bibles are just as dead as other books, are they not? Interesting, even inspiring, but dead.

So, both because of your logical unease about the relationship between Jesus the living Word and the Bible the written word, and also because of the emotional 'turn off' of a book, I start this third Bible reading at a disadvantage.

I can speak with warmth about our need to know God the Father, but what about the Bible? That is our challenge this morning.

I want us to begin with a most important section of John's Gospel. This marks the close of the public ministry of Jesus. In chapter 12:37–43 John teaches us why the public ministry of Jesus failed; and then in verses 44–50 he gives us a summary of the public ministry of Jesus, which divides into two halves. We shall see, I suggest, a rejected revelation (verses 37–43), a perfect revelation (verses 44–46), and finally a verbal revelation (verses 47–50). I want to spend most of our time on the last of these, for it will point to the answer: how does Jesus make the Father known today?

A rejected revelation

Why did the public ministry of Jesus fail? I put it provocatively. Perhaps we should ask, why did it not immediately succeed? Why at this stage did it seem to have failed? Because it certainly did seem that way. (We shall come back to this tomorrow when we consider the necessity and the wonder of the gracious ministry of God the Holy Spirit.)

There is, I think, one reason that is expressed in two ways. The reason is the scandal of the cross. This is precisely why, as we saw in chapter 6, the shallow euphoric enthusiasm for Jesus evaporated when he spoke of his broken body and out-poured blood. John teaches this first by two quotations from the prophet Isaiah. The first quotation in verse 38 is from Isaiah 53, that most famous passage about God's suffering servant dying a shameful death for the sins of the people. The second quotation comes from the end of the vision of Isaiah 6, because God chooses to blind the eyes of proud human beings to the revelation of his glory.

The connection between these two passages – from very different parts of Isaiah – is very striking. In each passage someone is 'high and lifted up' – the Lord in Isaiah 6 and the Servant in Isaiah 52:13. The visible glory of God in the vision of Isaiah 6 – God lifted up – is fulfilled in the strange glory of Isaiah 52 and 53, as the Servant is lifted up. In both these prophecies, Isaiah saw and grasped something of the true glory of Jesus, the one who, when he was lifted up, would shine with the clearest revelation of the glory of God (John 12:32, 33). This strange glory, this lifting-up on a cross, is so shocking that it is not surprising that proud human beings will not believe it. This is the scandal of the cross.

And then John illustrates this proud blindness with a fascinating cameo in verses 42–43. Astonishingly, 'many even among the leaders believed in [Jesus]'. They knew he was the Messiah; privately they would admit that. 'But because of the Pharisees they would not openly acknowledge their faith for fear that they would be put out of the synagogue [and therefore out of society]; for they loved human praise more than praise from God.' This is the scandal of walking in the footsteps of a crucified Messiah.

And so it is still. Our pride cannot stand the gospel of the cross. We love a successful Jesus and successful

Christians. We yearn to be great. We love the praise of people. There will always be something in the human heart – and even in professing Christian hearts – that rejects the revelation of the 'lifted up' Jesus. There is a real and necessary sense in which the public ministry of Jesus had to fail because of the scandal of the cross whose shadow fell on the Saviour from the start.

A perfect revelation

It was a rejected revelation and yet it was a perfect revelation. Verses 44–50 is John's summary of all of Jesus' public teaching. Like an epilogue it concludes and sums up the public ministry of Jesus rather as the great beginning in John 1:1–5 opened it. So, we may expect these seven verses to be of great significance. They are. There is a striking and simple structure to them. In verses 44–46 Jesus speaks about himself; seven times he says 'me' or 'I'. And then in verses 47–50 he speaks almost exclusively about his words. So let's start with Jesus himself.

Verses 44–46 sum up the great theme of the Gospel so far.

Whoever believes in me does not believe in me only, but in the one who sent me. The one who looks at me is seeing the one who sent me. I have come into the world as a light, so that no one who believes in me should stay in darkness.

To believe in Jesus is to believe in the Father. To look (with faith) at Jesus is to look at the Father. To believe and look with faith at Jesus is therefore to come out of the darkness of this world into the light that comes from the Father. Jesus makes the Father known. In those three years or so of public ministry there was, on display for all to see, the flawless revelation of the Father by the Son. For example, in chapter 3 as you watch the loving persuasion of Jesus to Nicodemus, the proud religious teacher, you see the loving persuasion of the Father. In chapter 11, as you watch the righteous anger of Jesus at the grave of Lazarus, you see the righteous anger of the Father. In those three years, Jesus, the Word made flesh, perfectly makes the Father known.

This revelation or 'making known' was right at the heart of all Jesus did. It was focused first on his apostles – 'I have revealed you *to those whom you gave me out of the world* . . . I have made you known *to them*' (John 17:6, 26). It is a wonderful thing that this unique group of apostolic eye-witnesses should be drawn into fellowship with the Father God through Jesus. Wonderful, that is, if you lived at the right time and in the right place. But there is a promise here which is even more wonderful. Jesus' prayer not only looks back ('I have made you known'); it also looks forward and promises, 'I . . . *will continue* to make you known' (John 17:26).

Jesus commits himself to continuing to make the Father known after he has left this earth. And this ongoing revelation of the Father is the only way that the love of God continues to break into a loveless and lost world. Jesus says to the Father that he will continue to make him known, 'in order that the love you have for me may be in them' (John 17:26). The love the Father has for Jesus is infinite, eternal and the source of all love. There is nothing more significant for the history of the world than for that love to overflow into men and women on earth.

A verbal revelation

And so we move from a rejected revelation and yet a perfect revelation to a verbal revelation. In verses 47–50 there is a very striking shift of focus from Jesus himself to his words. Although he continues to speak of himself, he now wants us to learn something about his words. At this point all our emotional coldness about words kicks in. But that theme of Jesus' words is not new. Have a look later through John's Gospel for the theme of Jesus as teacher – words like 'Rabbi', 'Teacher', 'word', 'words', 'teaching', 'testimony' and 'testify' abound. Teaching is what Jesus characteristically did.

In the prayer of John 17, Jesus says to the Father, 'I have revealed you to those whom you gave me out of the world . . . For *I gave them the words you gave me* and they accepted them' (John 17:6, 8, emphasis added). Even at his trial the high priest questioned Jesus about his disciples and his teaching. And before Pontius Pilate, Jesus says: 'the reason I was born and came into the world is to testify to the truth' (John 18:37). When John recounts the wonder of the apostolic testimony at the start of his first letter, he begins, 'That which was from the beginning, which we have heard' (1 John 1:1). He goes on to the fact that they saw, looked upon and touched. But he begins with what they heard. So there is this massive emphasis on Jesus' words. The physical, bodily, incarnate Jesus is no longer present on earth. But his words continue. And so I want us to take a step back and reflect on the words of Jesus.

How did Jesus of Nazareth make the Father known during his earthly life and ministry? If making the Father known was at the heart of his reason for coming to earth, it is important to know the answer. It was not by his physical appearance. Nor was it the miracles on their own, for they needed explanation. John characteristically speaks of Jesus' miracles as 'signs', because they were signposts pointing to his identity and work. And they were only signposts because of the words that accompanied them. The feeding of the 5,000 was ambiguous without the discourse of John 6. The raising of Lazarus had to be interpreted by words in John 11. Even his death on the cross only revealed the Father because it was interpreted by words. Many men were crucified by the Romans. It is only the words that surround this crucifixion that enable us to understand what it reveals and achieves. So, Jesus made the Father known by his words.

Before we consider what Jesus says about his words, I want us to take a step back and ask the question: Where do we hear the words of Jesus today? I'm going to give you a skeleton answer in three parts: the apostles, the New Testament and the Old Testament.

1. The apostles give reliable, Spirit-inspired testimony to Jesus

The first line is from Jesus Christ to his apostles. Jesus chose
the apostles to be with him throughout his public ministry,
that they might give reliable historical testimony to the
revelation of the Father by the Son. In the unique apostolic
band we have a hand-picked group of men, prayerfully
selected by Jesus to be with him and to be eye-witnesses
(between them) of the whole of his earthly ministry, death
and resurrection. They were to see the Father made known.
Further, he promised them a special and wonderful
ministry of the Holy Spirit after his departure, by which
they would be accurately reminded of the revelation they
had seen, given a full and perceptive understanding of it,
and led by the same Spirit into all the truth of Jesus. The
purpose of this human preparation and divine provision
was that the revelation of the Father in Jesus might be
passed on to us in a way that is utterly trustworthy.

Jesus clearly expected that this is what would happen.
He said to his apostles that, 'If they obeyed my teaching,
they will obey yours also' (John 15:20). Jesus says that
the response to the apostles' teaching is the same as the
response to his own teaching. He knew that when the time
came for them to be on their own, their teaching would be
his teaching, in its entirety and utter faithfulness, and that
their words would precisely have the meaning and force of
his words.

There is a beautiful little hint of this in John's Gospel. In
John 1:18 we read that because the Son is 'in the closest

relationship with' the Father, he makes the Father known. In older Bible translations we read 'in the bosom of' the Father. It conveys here an intimate closeness such that the Son can, with absolute reliability, make the Father known. It's not a very common Greek word. And it comes only one other time in John, in John 13:23 where the anonymous 'disciple whom Jesus loved' (we would say, 'Jesus' closest friend') is reclining at the Last Supper – and the NIV says 'next to' Jesus. The ESV has 'at Jesus' side'. It is literally, 'in the bosom of' Jesus, that is, with his head resting back on Jesus' chest, which is how it was if you were reclining next to someone at a supper. Just a hint, but the kind of hint in which John delights: Jesus can make the Father known because he is very close to him. And you can trust this apostle – you can trust all the apostles – because they were very close to Jesus.

2. We have that testimony in its final form in the New Testament

'This is the disciple who testifies to these things and *who wrote them down*,' says John at the end of his Gospel (21:24). It was recognized that the apostolic testimony needed to be written down. The New Testament is 'the apostolic collection': some were written by apostles, others written by those in the apostolic circle. For example, there is an early and probably reliable tradition that, in the second Gospel, Mark records the preaching of the apostle Peter. When Mark's Gospel began to circulate and be accepted, there were plenty of people alive who had heard the preaching of Peter. These people recognized that Mark's account was a trustworthy recording of that preaching. Luke tells us that he is recording the testimony of 'those who from the first were eye-witnesses and servants of the word', which must primarily mean the apostles, although for his birth and infancy narrative it seems that Luke drew also on the testimony of Mary the mother of Jesus. Those who read Luke and Acts recognized that Luke had indeed 'carefully investigated everything from the beginning' and written an account that gives us access to 'the certainty' of the Gospel of Jesus (Luke 1:1–4). Indeed, when he starts the book we call The Acts of the Apostles he hints that it contains what Jesus continued to do and to teach. For when the apostles taught, Jesus continued to teach.

Of course all sorts of pious writings began to circulate in the early church, and we have access to a number of them. But the criterion for them to be recognized as Scripture, and included later in the New Testament canon, was apostolicity, either authorship by an apostle directly or authorship by someone in the apostolic circle who was recognized as having faithfully recorded the apostolic teaching. Those who recognized the trustworthiness of the documents now included in our New Testament were originally those who were contemporary with the apostles.

It is because the New Testament is the apostolic collection of writings, recorded by apostles or by others under the supervision of the Spirit, that we may confidently affirm and trust that every New Testament word is the word of Jesus, and therefore the Word by which the Father is made known today. Jesus said he would continue to make the Father known; he does so by his words. We have those words, recorded with their exact force, meaning, balance and entirety, in the whole of the New Testament.

3. Jesus and his apostles affirm the inspiration and reliability of the whole Old Testament as the testimony of the Father, by the Spirit, to the Son

The Old Testament is not in any simple or historical sense 'the words of Jesus'. Here it is necessary to come at the problem from a different angle, and to see the Old Testament as God the Father's testimony by God the Spirit to God the Son. The following three observations may be made.

a. Jesus quotes the Old Testament as the Word of God, and he acknowledges its authority in his life and in his teaching. He is shaped and taught by it. It sets the agenda for his ministry.

b. The Old Testament makes Jesus intelligible and Jesus makes the Old Testament intelligible. It prepares us for him, and he completes it. As the writer to the Hebrews begins his letter, God has been speaking, and now he has spoken his final word.

c. Jesus taught that the Old Testament is the Father's testimony by the Spirit to the Son.

The line from 'the words of Jesus' to the words of the Bible is a sure and certain line.

Now we return to verses 47–50. I want us to note the following concerning Jesus' words: their eternal weightiness, their divine origin, their life-giving wonder and their enduring stability.

1. The eternal weightiness of Jesus' words

There is a paradox in verses 47 and 48. Jesus did not come into the world to judge the world but to rescue it. His mission was a rescue mission not a punishment mission. And yet, 'There is a judge for the one who rejects me and does not accept my words; the very words I have spoken will condemn them at the last day.' It would be hard to give greater weight to words than this: these words will be the accusing prosecutor and condemning judge on the last day, for all who reject them, and thereby reject Jesus. And then Jesus gives a reason. His words have eternal weightiness because they are of divine origin. So we notice next . . .

2. The divine origin of Jesus' words

Verse 49 underlines the origin of Jesus' words as coming from God the Father. There are two dimensions to this. On the one hand, the words of Jesus have their origin in eternity. Jesus is the Word who is God with God from all eternity (1:1, 2); he is the eternal and perfect self-expression of the truthful God, whose word perfectly expresses his nature, purposes and character. They are the words of the Father because Jesus is the eternal Son of the Father.

But, second, John makes it clear that the way Jesus learned those words in his full humanity was by the Holy Spirit. Jesus did not have them, as it were, by some supernatural hard-wiring in his brain because had he had that short-cut, he would not be like us, not fully human. No, he learned them from the Old Testament Scriptures, by the ministry of the Holy Spirit who was constantly with him. The Holy Spirit came upon him at his baptism and 'remained' (1:32–34). The Holy Spirit was the constant and intimate companion of Jesus from his conception, through his childhood, and then coming upon him with enabling power at his baptism, and on through every moment of his life on earth.

And in a very significant comment in chapter 3:31–36, probably a comment by John the Gospel-writer, John says this: 'For the one whom God has sent [Jesus] speaks the words of God, for God gives the Spirit without limit.' Everywhere else in the Bible the Spirit is given in some measure to human beings. But in this one case, he is given without limit – a limitless, boundless filling of the Spirit for the Son. And for this reason, this boundless Spirit-work, Jesus speaks exactly, perfectly and always the very words of God. And so the origin of Jesus' words is this: they are the words of God the Father from all eternity, and they are given to the man Christ Jesus by the limitless ministry of God the Holy Spirit. The three persons of the Holy Trinity work together to make the words of Jesus precisely the revelation of the Father by the Spirit.

3. The life-giving wonder of Jesus' words

Verse 50, 'I know that his command leads to eternal life.' Jesus speaks what God commands, and what he commands – which is the gospel – leads men and women to eternal life. This is why rejection of that Word must inevitably lead to judgment, for it is a turning-away from the only pathway to eternal life.

Jesus says in John 6:63: 'The words I have spoken to you – they are full of the Spirit and life.' In his excellent book, *Words of Life: Scripture as the Living and Active Word of God*, Dr Timothy Ward rightly suggests that the Father gave Jesus these words in eternity, that is that these words open to us something of 'the communicative activity that exists between the persons of the Trinity'. In which case, as Ward points out, it is not surprising that they are quite literally 'full of the Spirit', the breath of God himself. 'For how could words that have their origin in God and that God names as his own be anything else?'[2] These words of Jesus – anticipated in the words of the Old Testament written by the Spirit of Christ, fulfilled in the New Testament apostles, again by the Spirit of Christ – are the overflow on earth of the life and love of the Holy Trinity in eternity. They are Spirit-filled and therefore life-giving.

So here are words that have eternal weightiness (for we shall be judged by them), that have divine origin (which is why they are so weighty), and – also because of their divine origin – have a life-giving wonder. But I want us to notice one other feature.

4. The enduring stability of Jesus' words
Why this huge emphasis on words at the very end of Jesus' public ministry? Why this striking shift from the visible

person of Jesus in verses 44–46 to the words of Jesus in verses 47–50? I think the answer is this: Jesus will no longer be here, in his physical human body. So if the gospel is that the Father is made known by the incarnate Jesus, it would be a gospel only for those relatively few who lived in the right place and the right time. Clearly the physical appearance of Jesus was of no significance, which is why physical representations of him are always so unsatisfactory. Even his miracles were not of enduring significance on their own, for we were not there to witness them. The words of Jesus become the enduring and enduringly stable revelation of the Father on earth. They cannot be changed. They are trustworthy and true. They do not shift with the passing fashions of culture.

Jesus' words and the Bible

There are far-reaching ramifications to our answer to the question: how are the words of Jesus heard today? If we cannot answer it, then it is hard to see how Jesus' promise to go on and on making the Father known can be honoured. There are essentially only two kinds of answer we can give. Either we hear Jesus speaking in an interior, subjective, mystical way, or we hear Jesus speaking through the written and preached words of the Bible.

To put it another way, the question is about the connection between Jesus the Eternal Word and the written words of the Bible. When we speak loosely of 'the Word' there is this ambiguity. Do we mean the second person of the Trinity, the Eternal Word, Jesus Christ, or do we mean Scripture? Are we speaking of the Word who is a person, or of the Word that is words in a book?

At this point a division often appears between those who just assume that 'the Word' does mean Scripture (this being a generally untested assumption) and those who assume that 'the Word' means Jesus rather than the Bible (this assumption involves a generally unexamined doubt about Scripture). But neither this untested assumption nor this unexamined doubt will suffice. We need to examine and test this connection.

There are many who wish to prise apart the Eternal Word and the scriptural words. So, for example, the retired Oxford scholar John Barton writes, 'it is not primarily the Bible that is the Word of God, but Jesus Christ'. We must not, 'commit . . . bibliolatry: the elevation of the Bible above Christ himself . . . Christians are not those who believe in the Bible, but those who believe in Christ.'³ Many church leaders have had the same said to them, perhaps less eloquently, but just as disconcertingly. How unsettling it is to be told that we are unspiritual for insisting on Bible teaching being at the heart of church life, or that by so doing we are substituting a dead book for the living experience of a person. It sounds so pious when people say this to us. Who would not prefer a living person to printed words on a page? Who would want to be accused of worshipping a book? But I believe the accusation is unfounded and ultimately denies the power of the authentic Christ.

They used to say, slightly disparagingly, that at the height of the British Empire missionaries would go out with a sword or gun in one hand and a Bible in the other. While there may have been some truth in that, in the best instances there was no sword or gun, but only a Bible. There is no sword in the hand of mission partners today, whatever the country or ethnic group they come from, and wherever they go. The danger is that we abandon, not only the sword, but also the Bible; that we lose our confidence in the Bible. But the Bible has the authority of the words of Jesus. That Word will be our judge on the last day, and it can lead us to eternal life. Jesus was sent to speak those words to make the Father known. The Bible is the written testimony to those words.

Let us rejoice in our Bibles – what a treasure!

Let us get to know our Bibles – what a joy!

Let us use our Bibles – what a task!

Notes

1. Helmut Thielicke, *The Prayer that Spans the World: Sermons on the Lord's Prayer* (James Clarke, 1960), p. 21.

2. Timothy Ward, *Words of Life: Scripture as the Living and Active Word of God* (IVP, 2009).

3. John Barton, *People of the Book? The Authority of the Bible in Christianity* (SPCK, 2011).

The Spirit: sent to make the Son known (John 15:18 – 16:15)

Mission is hard. Some here are bruised, battered and discouraged in mission. Many of us feel like failures. I want to begin with the question we asked yesterday from John 12: why did Jesus fail? Why, even after Jesus had performed so many signs in their presence, did the people still not believe in him (12:37)? It was not an unexpected failure, for it was clearly prophesied. It was a necessary failure. Jesus expected it. He knew it must be so. And, of course, it was not a final failure! And yet, even after a perfect revelation of the Father, they did not believe. He came to his own, and his own did not receive him (John 1:11). Why?

We need to explore why Jesus failed, for it has a deep impact on our subject of Jesus making the Father known today. And it will help us to understand why mission is hard. Only after his earthly ministry was ended did people believe and understand. Suddenly, in their thousands and then millions, a multitude that no man can number, they believed. So what had changed? Before we find hope, our search will inject much-needed sober realism into our subject, for it speaks to us of our helplessness, our deep darkness and our utter inability to find the Father God for ourselves.

I want to divide our passage into five parts.

The Spirit and persecution (15:18–25)

The Holy Spirit is given to the church under pressure from a hostile world. Verse 18, 'If the world hates you . . .' The Greek construction means, 'If the world hates you, which it does and will.' 'Keep in mind [know for sure, be quite certain and never forget] that it hated me first' – first in time (chronologically before it hated you), but also first in primacy. 'It hated me as the defining object of its hatred.' Jesus spells out at least three dimensions of this hatred.

You will be hated because:

1. People want you to join them in hating God

Notice how 'the world' is named five times in verse 19. If you belonged to the world, it would love you as its own. The world does have a kind of love but it is different from the kind of love within the church. It is a love for 'its own', a circumscribed love, the love of a club for its members. The world hates the church because the church consists of men and women who used to belong to the world, but no longer do. We are traitors to the cause of godlessness. We have deserted the comfortable life of wickedness. We are former rebels who have been won back to the king. And therefore we are hated with a peculiar hatred by those who continue to rebel, because we have played them offside, we show them up (1 Peter 4:3–4).

2. People hate God

We are servants of a new master. We serve on a new team. We have been transferred. We represent him now. This is the flip-side of no longer belonging to the world. So, 'If they persecuted me [which they did], they will persecute you also. If they obeyed my teaching [as a few did], they will obey yours also. They will treat you this way because of my name [all I am, and all I represent], for they do not know the one who sent me' (verses 20–21).

The apostles are marked as 'Jesus' men, and therefore as 'God the Father' men, since he is 'the one who sent me'. They are marked men because at the heart of the world is a hatred of God. There is much kindness and goodness in the world, by the common grace of God. But at the heart of the mindset of the world is the desire to live in God's world without God, without the constraints of his law, without the constraining truths of his Word. And, therefore, the closer we stand to Jesus the more people's reactions to us express their heart reaction to Jesus, which is their response to the Father.

3. People are wicked

The point of verses 22–25 is that when a sinless man comes into the world and we hate him, it proves that our hatred is utterly inexcusable. When I dislike someone, I can always find something flawed about them to justify my dislike. But when pure and perfect goodness walks this earth and we hate him, there is no excuse. In a sense, 'they would not be guilty of sin' (verse 22) if Jesus hadn't come; that is, their guilt would not be evident, provable, incontrovertible. But Jesus' presence among them renders their sin inexcusable. Their hatred of Jesus is proof positive of their hatred of the Father. He lived a life of pure goodness and they hated him, proving their wickedness.

If the world hates Jesus they will most certainly hate his apostles and the apostolic church. For with us the unjustified hatred is mixed with all sorts of justified dislikes. So what possible chance is there of success in mission? None, it would seem! And so that brings us to the question: who will persuade men and women of the truth of Jesus? How can people possibly be persuaded?

The Spirit and the apostles (15:26, 27)

In verses 26–27 Jesus speaks of two witnesses. There is the witness or testimony of the Holy Spirit to Jesus, and there is the witness of the apostles to Jesus. Why both? Why is it not enough that God the Holy Spirit should bear witness to God the Son? After all, the Spirit is God. Is the testimony of God insufficient? Why must the apostles bear witness in addition to his testimony?

It seems a bit like saying to me, 'The Wimbledon champion needs a bit of help. Would you go on court to play beside him, and you can help him win?' It would be nonsense. I might as well sit by the court sipping lemon barley water for all the good I could do. If God the Holy Spirit is going to bear witness to Jesus, why do the apostles need to bother? It makes no sense unless their testimony and the Spirit's testimony are of different kinds, unless he is not supplementing their incompleteness with more of the same, but complementing their testimony with a different kind of witness. And this is exactly what he does.

The reason the apostles need to bear witness is that they were eye-witnesses, able to testify that the bodily incarnation of Christ is the revelation of the invisible Father (1 John 1:1–3). The Father was not made known through a non-bodily experience, a mystical experience, a vision, dream or inner perception; he was revealed by the bodily presence of Jesus Christ. Christianity is about an objective historical appearing. Those three years of Jesus' public ministry were and are and will always be the unique and defining moment of all history. Christianity is about objective truth. Questions of truth are less prominent today than once they were, but the question, 'Is it true?' won't go away. It is the only question which provides an anchor through the storms of life. You can have fake truth and half-truth, post-truth and untruth, but one day you will come face to face with true truth. Christianity is true truth.

It is worth pausing to reflect on the importance of those words: 'And you also must testify, for you have been with me from the beginning' (verse 27). The testimony of the apostles to the complete revelation of the Father in the earthly ministry of Jesus, from his anointing with the Spirit at his baptism until his ascension, is essential to anchor and root Christianity in history and objective truth. Without this anchor, Christianity metamorphoses into a subjective mystical experience with a vaguely Christian flavour. The transition from experience anchored in history into fluid mystical experience is not always easy to spot. But it marks a paradigm shift and it signals the abandonment of truth.

It is frightening how easily we Christians give others the impression that they ought to leave their minds at the church door and slip into mysticism. 'It's the feelings that matter', we say or imply. An example from Christian history that illustrates the importance of this objective truth is the debates between the so-called Puritans and the emerging Quaker movement in the seventeenth century. The Quakers began as Puritans who were dissatisfied with their experience of God. They were frustrated by church structures, found the Bible a cold and dead book, and longed for something more. The root question was, 'How does God speak?' Or, as we might say, 'What is the relationship between the Spirit and the Word? Is the Bible the Spirit's sword and book, or does the Spirit speak immediately to the individual apart from the Bible?' And it is sobering to see how Quakerism developed. They began with a longing for experience, but soon they denied that God spoke through the Bible at all and went far away from anything that could be called historic Christianity. Before long they had cut the anchor to historical truth and apostolic testimony.

Christian faith begins with the objective fact of Jesus Christ and our experiences are meaningless apart from him. This is why Jesus' apostles had to testify. In a moment we will ask what sort of testimony the Holy Spirit will give (verses 8–15). We've looked at the Spirit and persecution; the Spirit and the apostles; now . . .

The Spirit and the cross (16:1–7)

Verse 7, 'Very truly I tell you, it is for your good that I am going away. Unless I go away, the Advocate will not come to you; but if I go, I will send him to you.' When Jesus talks about 'going' he means going to the cross. Only when Jesus has been lifted up, glorified, at the cross can the Spirit be poured out as living water to give new birth. Why? I think the answer is this. We think it would be a wonderful thing if the Spirit of the living God would come into our hearts. But actually it would mean instant death. For burning holiness to enter my sinful heart would burn me up. Until my sin is paid for. Until Jesus is glorified on the cross. Jesus tells the apostles that it is for their good that he is going away to the cross, to bear their sins. For only then will the Advocate, the Holy Spirit, come.

The Spirit and the world (16:8–11)

From verses 8–15 Jesus now tells us what is the testimony
of the Holy Spirit. If the apostles give historical eye-witness
testimony, what manner of witness does the Holy Spirit
bear to Jesus? Why is he sent by the Father and the Son?
The answer comes in two parts. The first part relates to the
ministry of the Spirit in the world. 'When he [the Spirit]
comes, he will prove the world to be in the wrong [convict
the world] about sin and righteousness and judgment'
(verse 8). The Spirit has a ministry and testimony of conviction. By nature the world will not believe; none of us
will until the Holy Spirit convicts us. The Spirit is not
guiding the world. He is not leading the world into truth
or working in other religions. His ministry is not to affirm
the world; it is to show the world that the world is wrong.
The only work the Bible says the Spirit of God does in the
world is to bring conviction. He takes the objective
historical apostolic testimony to Jesus and places it against
the unbelieving heart.

He brings conviction of sin, 'because people do not
believe in me' (verse 9). This probably means not just
that unbelief in Jesus is a sin but that unbelief in Jesus
proves and exposes sin (as we saw in 15:22–25). If a
prophet speaks to me, I can always find some reason for
rejecting what he says. Always there is something wrong
with the preacher or the messenger, and so I can find an
excuse for ignoring them. But when a perfect man
preaches to me and I reject and hate him, I show that I

have no excuse and my sin is exposed. Jesus is proof-positive of our guilt.

Second, he brings a conviction about righteousness 'because I am going to the Father' (verse 10). The world thought Jesus was unrighteous, and that is why they crucified him. But when he goes to the Father, the world's verdict is turned upside down and it is publicly seen that Jesus is righteous. The Spirit convicts the world that Jesus is righteous, and therefore, by implication, that we are not.

Third, he brings conviction about judgment 'because the prince of this world now stands condemned' (verse 11). The prince of this world, Satan, who stands at the pinnacle of all this world's value systems, is shown up to be utterly evil and condemned, when he crucifies the righteous Jesus. By nature I thought the world's values were valid and I took my values from the world. The Spirit convinces me how utterly wrong I was.

We see this convincing and convicting work in evidence in the young church in Thessalonica. Paul writes:

> For we know, brothers and sisters loved by God, that he
> has chosen you, because our gospel came to you not simply
> with words but also with power, with the Holy Spirit and
> deep conviction.
> (1 Thessalonians 1:4–5)

The gospel of Jesus did come in words (it always does); but it did not come 'simply with words'. Those words were accompanied by the necessary and complementary work of the Spirit who first brought the gospel to bear on the hearts of the preachers, so that they themselves were deeply convinced that their message was true. And then he brought their words to bear on their hearers. He convinced people through convinced people. This is the work of the Spirit. He does not add fresh information beyond the apostolic gospel, but he persuades men and women that this gospel is true.

The ministry of the Holy Spirit is to take what seems true in an outward sense and to make it true in an inward sense, to make it real in experience. There is no real Christian experience apart from the ministry of the Holy Spirit. He is 'the Spirit of truth'. We cannot do this convincing work for ourselves or for others by our preaching, our witness, our apologetics, or our lives. People can be completely untouched by everything Christians say and do. Only the Spirit can bring this conviction.

So this convicting work is the ministry of the Holy Spirit in the world. But there is another context in which the Spirit bears testimony to Jesus Christ:

The Spirit and the Church (16:12–15)

In John 16:12–15 Jesus makes the apostles another promise. These verses begin with a puzzle: 'I have much more to say to you, more than you can now bear.' In John 15:15 Jesus says that the apostles are his friends and that 'everything' he has learned from the Father he has already 'made known' to them. He has not just given them the first instalment of an ongoing serial revelation of the Father; he has given them the full revelation of the Father.

So, what can he mean by saying that he has 'much more' to say to them? The point of John 15:15 is the open relationship of trust. Jesus doesn't hold back secret things from them and only give them the documents not marked 'top secret'. They have, as it were, the highest level of security clearance for access to God's truth. But although they have this security clearance they simply cannot cope with it all at once. They can't 'bear' it. It is rather like when the Fraud Squad raid a company's offices, and we see them on television carrying out box loads of papers. In one sense, they have all the information from that day on. But they cannot 'bear' it yet, and it will take many months of unpacking and working through the material before they can issue their report. There is simply too much to absorb at once.

In a similar way, it is not that Jesus gradually gives the apostles more access to the revelation of the Father. It is that the process of learning will take a lifetime, and therefore they will need a lifetime tutor as they, as it were, work through the revelation of the Father in Jesus. And the Spirit is that lifetime tutor for the apostles. The Spirit does not add to the final word of Jesus; rather he unpacks that word for the apostles. He will not give them extra little presents of revelation arriving day by day in the heavenly hotline post, gradual downloads or updates (as we might get over the Internet for updating a programme). Rather, he tutors them in the gradual unpacking of the one great present they have already been given.

People sometimes suggest that the Spirit works on a kind of parallel track to the Bible. The Bible reveals Christ and then, separately and independently, the Spirit reveals. This must be wrong. For the revelation of the Father given by Jesus is complete. Jesus Christ was not the start of a revelatory process; he was and is the revelatory event. Any suggestion of supplementary and consequential revelations inevitably detracts from the fullness and sufficiency of the Father made known by the Son.

So what will the Holy Spirit do? Jesus goes on to promise, 'He will guide you into all the truth' (John 16:13). The word 'guide' comes from the same root as the word 'way' (as in John 14:6 'I am the way . . .'). When he comes, he will 'way' you into all truth, lead you in the way and the truth. He will guide you to walk with and like Jesus. To be guided into truth is not primarily to be told facts. Truth in the New Testament is much deeper than knowing things, although it is never less. Truth is relationship with a person, the Lord Jesus who is the truth. To know the truth is to know the authentic Jesus and therefore to know the Father. Furthermore, truth is not merely something that is 'known' in a head-knowledge sense; truth is something which is done. I do not know truth so much as do truth. To be led into the truth is to be led into relationship with Jesus and to walk with Jesus, in his footsteps, to walk as he walked.

Now, in the first instance, this promise is given to the apostles, and it is very important to begin with this primary meaning. Jesus does not directly say to us or the church today, 'the Spirit will lead *you* into all the truth.' He promised the apostles that the Spirit would lead *them* into all truth, just as in John 14:26 he reminds the apostles of all he had spoken, and teaches them what it means. It is common to suggest that Jesus promises that the Holy Spirit will go on and on leading the church into more and more truth, in the sense of helping us to realize there have been things we have got wrong, and enabling us to get them right. The Jerusalem Council of Acts 15 is often suggested as a model for this. The church agreed unitedly for the first time that Gentile believers in Christ would be admitted into Christ's church on the basis of faith alone, with no requirements to come under the law of Moses. When sending their decision out from Jerusalem, the Council famously included the words, 'It seemed good to the Holy Spirit and to us . . .' (Acts 15:28). So, it is suggested, Synods and Councils of the church today may expect the same kind of leading.

But although helpful lessons may be learned from Acts 15 about Christian decision-making, the chapter is not a paradigm for church decisions today. It would be a serious mistake to think that a Synod or Council of the church today can make a change to Christian doctrine or ethics and preface it with the words, 'It seemed good to the Holy Spirit and to us.' For this decision in Acts is part of the fulfilment of Jesus' promise to the *apostles* that the Holy Spirit would lead *them* into all truth, unpacking for them the complete revelation of the Father in Christ. The inclusion of the Gentiles was one very significant out-working of the great event of Jesus Christ. Paul repeatedly refers to it as 'the mystery of Christ' which had been hidden, but in the gospel is now revealed (see Ephesians 3:2–3 and Colossians 1:26). The Spirit revealed to Paul that the Gentile mission of the church was the necessary outworking of what Jesus Christ had done on earth. But when the apostolic era came to an end with the death of the last apostles, that ministry of the Spirit to the apostles was completed. He had indeed led the apostles into all truth, and we have that complete and sufficient deposit of truth in the apostolic collection we call the New Testament.

The promise Jesus makes is strongly Trinitarian. Just as Jesus never spoke 'on his own', that is, independently of the Father who sent him (John 7:16–18; 8:26,28; 12:49; 14:10), so the Spirit 'will not speak on his own' but will speak 'only what he hears', that is, what he hears from the Father and the Son (John 16:13). His ministry is to lead the apostles into the full understanding of the completed revelation of the Father in the earthly life, teaching, miracles, death and resurrection of Jesus Christ.

But what does Jesus mean by saying, 'and he will tell you what is yet to come' (John 16:13)? Is this not a promise of future and additional revelations? Let us look closely at the argument. Unfortunately the NIV disguises a verbatim repetition between verses 13 and 14:

he will tell you [literally, 'declare to you'] what is yet to come.
(verse 13)

it is from me that he will receive what he will make known
to you [literally, 'declare it to you'].

(verse 14)

The repetition of 'declare to you' strongly suggests that
the subject of the first declaration, 'what is yet to come', is
linked with the subject of the second declaration, 'what
is mine'. Just as Jesus declared to the apostles the things of
the Father, and so made the Father known, so the Spirit
will declare to them the things of Jesus, and so make Jesus
known, and therefore the Father known. Since 'all that
belongs to the Father' belongs also to Jesus, when the Spirit
takes the things of Jesus and makes them known, by doing
so he simultaneously makes the Father known.

So, it would seem that the things that are 'yet to come'
are in some way connected to the things of Jesus. They are
the future implications of the things of Jesus. The Spirit is
not promised to give them a kind of time-traveller insight
into future events at random, in some simple predictive
sense. He will teach them the implications of Jesus Christ
for the future. This would include what it means to live
under the new covenant. For example, he taught them
how Jews and Gentiles live together, all justified by faith
alone (as the Spirit revealed to Peter in Acts 10). He showed
them how the temple is replaced and all the shadows and
signs of Old Testament Judaism are fulfilled in Jesus (as in
Hebrews, for example). He revealed how Israel the people
of God ceases to be a political kingdom and becomes an
international church, Jew and Gentile (as in Matthew,

Galatians or Romans). He will teach them the implications of Christ's death and resurrection, looking forward to his second coming, the final judgment and his world lordship.

This is what we find, even in the book of Revelation, which is given 'to show [Christ's] servants what must soon take place' (Revelation 1:1) and yet consists not of simple predictions of the future, but rather, in apocalyptic style, of the unpacking of the implications of Christ for the present and future. Everything that results from, and is implied and caused by, the great event of the Word becoming flesh, the Spirit unpacked for the apostles over the years that followed. This is exactly what we find in the apostolic writings – not a random collection of predictive prophecies, but a coherent, Christ-centred, exposition of the past, present and future in the light of the revelation of the Father in Jesus Christ.

The Spirit will bring glory to Jesus (John 16:14). Just as Jesus sought the Father's glory, so the Spirit seeks Jesus' glory. He takes the things of Jesus ('what is mine'), the grace and kindness of God given to us in and through Jesus, and makes them known, so that men and women may know, obey, love and worship Jesus. He is, if we may put it like this, the person of the Trinity who most likes to remain invisible. He does not draw attention to his own ministry, but brings glory to Jesus, who makes the Father known.

And as he does that, all the intimacy of the Son and the Father are brought into play. What are the things of Jesus?

They are the things that belong to the Father – all of them.
All that belongs to the Father belongs to Jesus. The things
of the Holy Spirit are without exception the things that
belong to Jesus and therefore the things that belong to the
Father (John 16:15). So just as the Spirit brings conviction
into the world about our sinfulness, and the righteousness
of Jesus, and the defeat of Satan, so he leads the apostolic
church in the way of the apostles, which is the way of
Jesus, which is the way of the Father. He does not lead us
beyond the apostolic revelation of Jesus, for the apostolic
revelation of Jesus is true and complete. But he leads us in
it. A Spirit-led church will be a Bible-driven church, a
church submitting gladly to the authority of the Bible in
both teaching and lifestyle.

So, what was necessary before the ministry of Jesus
could bear fruit? First, the cross, so that sins would be paid
for. And second, the outpouring of the Spirit, so that the
world would begin to be convicted of sin, righteousness
and judgment, and so that the apostolic church would
begin to be led in the way of Jesus, which is the way of the
Father. This is why at the end of Jesus' public ministry in
John 12 there is almost total failure. There had to be. There
was always going to be. Jesus knew and expected that. And
it is why, after the cross, the resurrection, the ascension
and the outpouring of the Spirit at Pentecost, the ministry
of Jesus began to draw millions upon millions to the Father,
from all over the world. The Holy Spirit was sent by the
Father and the Son to bear testimony to Jesus, to bring
the objective apostolic testimony to bear upon reluctant

human hearts, so that we put up our hands and admit we are wrong, and so that the church of Christ begins to walk in the way of Christ, which is the way of the Father, which is the way of the Bible testimony.

The Spirit is sent to a church under pressure. He complements the historical testimony of the apostles with the inward testimony of conviction and leading into apostolic truth. He comes only because sin has been paid for at the cross. He convicts the world of sin and leads the church in the way of the apostles.

Praise God for the Holy Spirit, sent by the Father and the Son!

The Disciples: sent to bring life in Jesus' name (John 20:19–31)

The risen Jesus stands today, as he stands every day, in the midst of his church. And he says, 'As the Father has sent me, I am sending you' (John 20:21). Whoever you are, if you belong to Jesus, Jesus is sending you today. He is not simply sending young people. You may be retired: Jesus sends you – today.

We are nearly at the end of our convention week. It is a good time to ask, 'What next? How has what I have heard from the Word of God impacted me? What ought to be my priorities? To what should I direct such energies as God may give me at my stage of life? For what does Jesus send me? To whom? To do what? To say what?' The day will come when you and I stand before the risen and ascended Jesus and he says to us, 'I sent you. Did you go? Did you go to those to whom I sent you? Did you say and do what I sent you to say and do?'

I said on Monday that when people write about mission, often the only look-in that John's Gospel gets is these words in John 20:21. It has become a peg on which people hang whatever they think mission ought to be, a kind of talisman that gives an aura of Jesus to whatever we want to say about mission. But I want us to listen to it carefully this morning in the context in which Jesus said it, and in the light of all we have learned from the theme of 'sending' in John's Gospel. In this short passage we find five principles of mission as John's Gospel presents it to us. It is not the whole of the Bible's teaching, of course, but it is a significant part.

The sphere of mission is a world hostile to Jesus (John 20:19)

Come with me in your heart and mind and join the church of Christ behind locked doors. The doors are tight shut because they are terrified of the hostile Jewish leaders. Literally, John says, 'because of fear of the Jews'. They are all Jews, of course; all the disciples are Jews at this stage. But by his shorthand 'the Jews', John means the hostile Jewish leaders of the day, which is why the NIV now translates 'the Jews' as 'the Jewish leaders'.

We know from the parallel place in Luke 24 that those gathered on that first Easter evening are not just the eleven remaining apostles. When the two disciples on the Emmaus road go back to Jerusalem after meeting the risen Jesus, we read that, 'they found the Eleven *and those with them*, assembled together' (Luke 24:33). So this is a wider gathering; perhaps some of the loyal women were there, perhaps some other men too. We may think of it as the church of Christ in seed form on that first Easter evening.

They gather behind locked doors because the world outside is a hostile place. The world into which Jesus is about to send them is a place to which they would rather not go. And with good reason. 'If the world hates you,' Jesus had said – and there is no question that it will – 'keep in mind that it hated me first' (John 15:18).

If we say that the sphere of mission is the world, that can sound rather an exciting adventure. And in one sense it is. God so loved the world (John 3:16), the whole world, in all its diversity, grandeur, and richness of potential, with so many signs within it of the common grace and kindness of God, a place of beauty, kindness, loyalty and love. And yet in its deepest heart, the world is defined by hostility to Jesus and to the Father who sent him. John has signalled this right at the start:

> The true light that gives light to everyone was coming
> into the world. He was in the world, and though the world
> was made through him, the world did not recognise
> [acknowledge] him.
> (John 1:9–10)

'God so loved the world' – not that he smiled beneficently upon it with quiet approval, but 'that he gave his one and only Son, that whoever believes in him shall not *perish*'

(John 3:16), for that is otherwise the only destiny of the world apart from the grace of Christ. We have seen this hostility dramatically unfold as the pure goodness of Jesus arouses a bleak, dark, unrelenting hatred that climaxes at the cross.

> This is the verdict: light has come into the world, but people loved darkness instead of light because their deeds were evil. Everyone who does evil hates the light, and will not come into the light for fear that their deeds will be exposed.
> (John 3:19–20)

The world into which the risen Jesus sends his followers, the world beyond those locked doors, is not waiting to welcome us with open arms. It is a world by nature hostile to Jesus because it is hostile to the Father. This hostility is most intensely focused where there is religious zeal. It was the zeal of the Pharisees that drove the crucifixion of Jesus. It was the zeal of Saul of Tarsus and the Jewish Sanhedrin that fuelled the first great persecution, after the martyrdom of Stephen (Acts 8). This religious zeal may come from other religions. It may come from the zealous Hindu in India, the zealous Buddhist in East Asia, the zealous Muslim, the zealous Shinto devotee in Japan, or the zealous atheist, with the religious certainty that comes from the atheist faith.

The church of Christ needs to throw open the locked doors and go out. But they are not to go out because they have misread the world outside; it is not that they are dreaming that the world outside is hostile, when actually it is full of friendly faces. No! They are quite right in what they expect from the world outside, and they are to go out in spite of that. The sphere of mission is a world hostile to Jesus.

The instrument of mission is the joyful church of Jesus (John 20:19–21)

If the locked doors are the first thing we notice about the church, here our attention is gripped far more deeply by the appearance of the risen Lord. His substantial resurrection body walks through the locked door – not that his body is ghostly and the door is solid, but that by comparison with the solid substantiality of the resurrection body, the door is ghostly, insubstantial, a place of the shadowlands.

Verse 19, 'Jesus came and stood among them.' The risen Lord stands in the midst of his fearful church. As John will later see him in a vision, walking among the lampstands (Revelation 1), or figuratively on Mount Zion (Revelation 14), so now he stands in the midst of his people and says, 'Peace be with you!' He shows them his hands and his side – the marks, now fixed for eternity, of his crucifixion, not healing up like our scars, but for ever clear.

'The disciples were overjoyed when they saw the Lord' (verse 20). Now they begin to grasp that the Jesus they knew as teacher and master is the Lord, the Sovereign One to whom all authority in heaven and earth is given. And again he says, 'Peace be with you!' Twice the greeting of peace. Peace with God through his death. Peace now possible with one another. Peace offered to a world at war. Peace in the Father's love. Jesus had said just three evenings before, 'I have told you these things, so that in me you may have peace. In the world you will have trouble. But take heart! I have overcome the world' (John 16:33).

Before we consider things like the means, the message, the goal of mission, I want us to remember that the sending is not so much of isolated individuals as of a people. Jesus sends you and me only as members of his church. That church assembles – as we assemble this morning – with the risen Lord in our midst, the recipients of his peace and his joy. And then the Lord says, 'As the Father has sent me, I am sending you.' We have seen that there is a sending in the heart of the Father who sent the Son to die, to make the Father known. But from the beginnings of the Gospel we have seen hints that this sending will not end with the Son.

Chapter 1:37–45

Right back in chapter 1:37, two of John the Baptist's disciples (Andrew and probably John himself) begin to follow Jesus. Then Andrew finds his brother Simon and brings him to Jesus (John 1:41). Then Jesus finds Philip and Philip finds Nathanael (John 1:43, 45). And by chapter 2:12 we read of Jesus, 'with his mother and brothers *and his disciples*'. So there's the beginnings of the band of disciples. Why? What are they for? Are they just interested spectators? No!

Chapter 4:31–38

There is a most revealing hint in chapter 4. Jesus has met the Samaritan woman at the well; his disciples have gone into the town to buy food. They come back and urge Jesus to eat. And then Jesus, who has been alone, thirsty, outside a city wall, in the middle of the day, says to them, 'I have food to eat that you know nothing about . . . My food . . . is to do the will of him who sent me and to finish his work' (John 4:32, 34). Almost two years later he will again be alone, thirsty, outside a city wall, in the middle of the day, and will cry, 'It is finished!' (John 19:30). He will finish the work for which he was sent. That work will be completed. Nothing can be added, nothing need be added, to it.

Our mission is not the same as his mission, for his was a unique mission and he finished it. We cannot use this to prove that Christian mission must include physical healing, for example, good though that may be. For by the same logic Christian mission would necessarily have to include not only exorcisms but also raising of the dead, walking on water, stilling of storms or feeding huge crowds from a picnic box. No, our mission springs from his mission; but it cannot be the same.

So watch what happens next. Jesus says to his disciples, 'open your eyes and look at the fields! They are ripe for harvest . . . *I am sending* you to reap' (John 4:35–38, adapted). 'You are not simply here to follow me; you are here to be sent.' Immediately after this there is a wonderful work among the Samaritans, as the woman bears testimony to

Jesus, and many of them say, 'now . . . we know that this man really is the Saviour of the world' (John 4:42).

Chapter 7:35
And then, in the middle of chapter 7, there is some strange speculation about Jesus. He says he is going away. The people wonder whether he means he is going outside the Promised Land, to 'the Greeks', the Greek-speaking Gentiles in the rest of the world? It's a hint that is just left hanging there.

Chapter 10:16
In chapter 10 he speaks of having 'other sheep' that are not of this (Jewish) sheepfold; 'I must bring them also. They too will listen to my voice and there shall be one flock and one shepherd.'

Chapter 12:19, 20, 32
After the raising of Lazarus, the Pharisees lament that 'the whole world has gone after him' (John 12:19); immediately after which, 'some Greeks' (Greek-speaking Gentiles) come and ask to see Jesus (John 12:20). It is like the Magi in Jesus' infancy, representatives of the rest of the world, a hint and foretaste of a worldwide mission to come: 'I, when I am lifted up,' he says, 'will draw all people [all kinds of people] to myself' (John 12:32).

Chapter 13:20
In chapter 13:20 Jesus says to his apostolic church, 'Very truly I tell you, whoever accepts anyone I send accepts me;

and whoever accepts me accepts the one who sent me.' Jesus' point is, 'I am going to send. I am going to send with authority, so that those who believe the message of those I send receive me; and all who receive me receive the Father who sent me.'

Chapter 17:13–18
And then, in his great prayer, he prays this for the apostles:

> I am coming to you now, but I say these things while I am still in the world, so that they may have the full measure of my joy within them. I have given them your word and the world has hated them, for they are not of the world any more than I am of the world. My prayer is not that you take them out of the world but that you protect them from the evil one. They are not of the world, even as I am not of it. Sanctify them by the truth; your word is truth. As you sent me into the world, I have sent them into the world.
> (John 17:13–18)

So the authority for Christian mission is the sending of Jesus. And with his authority comes his prayer that his apostolic church will not be 'of the world'. When the locked doors are opened and the apostolic church goes out into the world, as it will on the day of Pentecost, it goes to remain distinctive, to be protected from the evil one, not to be of the world but to be sanctified by the truth of God's Word. The most dangerous threat that the world poses to the church is not persecution – it is assimilation. As one faithful eighteenth-century minister said, 'a kick from the world does believers less harm than a kiss'.[1]

The sphere of mission is a hostile world. The instrument of mission is the joyful church of Jesus. And . . .

The divine agent of mission is the Holy Spirit of Jesus (John 20:22)

'And with that he breathed on them and said, "Receive the Holy Spirit."' The words 'on them' are not in the original; it is just 'he breathed . . . and said . . .' This brings to its climax a great motif in John's Gospel.

Chapter 1:33
In chapter 1, John the Baptist says, with wonder, that he saw the Spirit of God come down upon Jesus at his baptism and 'remain' or 'abide' (John 1:33). The Spirit of God, the third person of the Trinity, the personal presence of God, was the intimate companion of Jesus throughout his life. But at his baptism, the start of his public ministry, the Spirit comes upon him in a fresh way to empower him. This man, says John the Baptist, 'is the one who will baptize with the Holy Spirit'. He will pour the personal presence of God into human hearts.

Chapter 4:10–14 and 7:37–39
In chapter 4 he offers the Samaritan woman 'living water'. In John 7:39 we learn that this living water speaks

of the Holy Spirit, who will be given after Jesus has been lifted up on the cross.

Chapter 19:30

On the cross as he dies, Jesus cries out, 'It is finished!' and immediately 'gave up his spirit', or – perhaps more literally – 'handed over his Spirit'.

So now he breathes out over his church and says, 'Receive the Holy Spirit.' I take it this is an anticipatory action, a symbol of what will become reality on the day of Pentecost. For it is only at Pentecost that the church begins to speak and act differently. This is the first thing Jesus says after sending them. You cannot be sent without the Spirit. Jesus says much the same at the start of Acts where he tells them, 'Do not leave Jerusalem, but wait for the gift my Father promised . . . you will be baptised with the Holy Spirit . . . You will receive power when the Holy Spirit comes on you; and you will be my witnesses' (Acts 1:4, 5, 8).

God the Holy Spirit is the divine agent of mission. He brings conviction of sin to the world – conviction of sin, of the righteousness of Jesus, of the judgment of the ruler of this world. He led the apostles into all truth so that the New Testament is the trustworthy testimony to Jesus; he leads the apostolic church into that truth into which he led the apostles, so that we learn and trust and submit to the authoritative and reliable testimony to Jesus that we have in the New Testament.

Their mission – our mission – is a spiritual mission; it is a mission in which the Holy Spirit will blow and change the hearts of men and women to give them new birth, as Jesus promised to Nicodemus in chapter 3. It is not at root a mission that brings transformation to society in this age. When men and women are given new birth, they will speak and act differently and their different behaviour will indeed transform their society, in some measure. But the transformation of society is not the heart of Christian mission, which is the transformation of the human heart, one by one by one. We cannot do this. Only the Spirit of God, who is the Spirit of Jesus, can change the human heart. We need to pray for his working in us, through us, among us, as we go where Jesus sends us.

The sphere of mission is a world hostile to Jesus. The instrument of mission is the church of Jesus – joyful, at peace with the crucified and risen Lord in our midst. The divine agent of mission is the Holy Spirit of Jesus – to empower us for testimony and to convict the world. Now we come to . . .

The message of mission is the forgiveness of sins through Jesus (John 20:23)

After the promise of the Holy Spirit, the first and only content of mission that Jesus explicitly gives concerns the forgiveness of sins: 'If you forgive anyone's sins, their sins are forgiven; if you do not forgive them, they are not forgiven' (verse 23). The removal of sins is a lot more important in the gospel than it is in much contemporary Christianity. When a man or woman tells their story of coming to faith, it is not very often that we hear the words, 'Wonderfully, my sins were forgiven. Never mind how I felt or what happened in my circumstances, the most deeply wonderful thing is that my sins were forgiven. I was a guilty sinner and now I am a forgiven sinner. I was weighed down with guilt, but now my burden has fallen from me.'

But what does Jesus mean when he says, 'If *you* forgive anyone's sins, their sins are forgiven; if *you* do not forgive them, they are not forgiven'? Is he giving to the individual Christian, or to some special Christians, the personal authority to forgive – or not forgive – sins? Two observations will help us unpack this. First, the people present were not just the apostles. Indeed one apostle, Thomas, was not present, as we are soon to discover (John 20:24). So no interpretation that focuses on the apostles alone will be persuasive. Even if we were to accept the Roman Catholic teaching that the apostolic laying on of hands provides an apostolic continuity between the apostles and the priesthood, we could not use this passage in that connection. And, of course, if the old tradition is correct that Thomas became the apostle to India, it would be a shame for Indian Christianity that the forgiveness of sins would not be available! No, this gathering is 'the Eleven [apostles] and those with them' (Luke 24:33); it is an unspecific sample of the whole church. Whatever Jesus meant, he meant for the whole of his church.

The second observation is that there is no evidence that the early church understood Jesus to be giving a personal authority to forgive sins. On the contrary, they understood their commission to be the proclamation of the forgiveness of sins in Jesus' name. As Jesus says in Luke 24:47, 'repentance for the forgiveness of sins will be preached in [the Messiah's] name to all nations.' That is to say, 'If you repent and trust in Jesus who died for sinners, your sins will be forgiven; if you do not, they will not.' This is an extraordinary, and authoritative, declaration that may be made by any Christian who knows the gospel. The point is this: the forgiveness of sins is central to the gospel and to the mission of the church. As forgiven sinners, we bring to a guilty world a message of extraordinary wonder: there is forgiveness of sins and it is to be found in Jesus' name, and in Jesus' name alone.

Now we turn to . . .

The method of mission is Scripture as testimony to Jesus (20:24–31)

In verses 24–29 we come to the question, 'How are men and women to *know* that these things are true?' The answer is that there are two ways they might know, and in the person of Thomas our passage sets them side by side.

The first way is by seeing, by sensory perception. There has been a lot of seeing in John 20 – Mary *sees* the stone has been removed (verse 1), John *looks* into the tomb (verse 5), Peter *looks* into the tomb (verse 6), John goes into the tomb, *sees* and believes (verse 8), Mary *looks* into the tomb and *sees* two angels (verses 11–12), she *sees* Jesus (verse 14), she says, 'I have *seen* the Lord' (verse 18), Jesus *showed* them his hands and side . . . they were overjoyed when they *saw* the Lord (verse 20).

So you can see the risen Lord. That's what the apostles did. You needed to see to be an apostle. At the start of his first letter, John said 'we' – that is, we apostles – 'have heard . . . seen with our eyes . . . looked at and our hands have touched . . . the Word of life' (1 John 1:1–3). There can be no apostles in that sense today. In the providence of God, one apostle, Thomas, was not there to see on that first Easter day. So the other disciples told him, 'We have *seen* the Lord!' (verse 25). I guess each of them said that every time they saw him. 'Hi, Thomas, we have seen the Lord!' . . . on Monday, Tuesday, Wednesday, Thursday, Friday, Saturday. Imagine the conversations. Imagine Thomas getting pretty fed up. 'I wish you'd shut up. I wish I'd seen the Lord. But I haven't.' Verse 25, 'Unless I *see* the nail marks in his hands and put my finger where the nails were, and put my hand into his side, I will not believe.'

And then Sunday comes. Again they are together, but this time Thomas is with them. Again, Jesus comes, stands, speaks: 'Peace be with you!' And then he turns to open-mouthed Thomas: 'Put your finger here; see my hands. Reach out your hand and put it into my side. Stop doubting and believe.' This is more of an invitation than a rebuke. Jesus gives Thomas the same sensory evidence for his resurrection that he has given the other apostles. Thomas believes: 'My Lord and my God!' He bows before the deity of God the risen Son.

And Jesus says, verse 29, 'Because you have seen me, you have believed.' Nothing wrong with that: that's why the others believed; that is the basis of apostolic belief – seeing him. But here's the new thing: 'Blessed are those who have not seen and yet have believed.' Thomas stands on the cusp of a new kind of faith. 'Thomas,' says Jesus, 'it is good you have seen and believed; it would have been even better if you had believed the others when they testified that they had seen. There would have been no less blessing in that. And that is going to be the basis of faith from now on.' When people become Christians now, it is not because they have seen the risen Jesus; it is not because they have had the Damascus Road experience that Paul had. They will believe, not because they themselves have seen the risen Jesus, but because they trust those who have.

And that's why John ends the chapter as he does, in verses 30–31:

> Jesus performed many other signs in the presence of his disciples, which are not recorded in this book. But these are written that you may believe that Jesus is the Messiah, the Son of God, and that by believing you may have life in his name.

You can see and believe; or you can believe those who saw. We instinctively think that seeing is best. But Jesus says blessed are those who do not see and yet believe – that is, believe those who did see, believe John, believe the apostles, read the New Testament and trust those who wrote it.

Read the book, believe, and find life in Jesus' name. Jesus has prayed for you too. In John 17:20 he says to his Father, 'My prayer is not for them alone [the apostles]. I pray also for those who will believe in me through their message.'

So the method of mission is to take the apostolic testimony, which is found in the New Testament, and the prophetic testimony found in the Old Testament – this perfect Spirit-inspired trustworthy testimony to Jesus – to take this Bible and bring its message to all who will hear.

To sum up, the sphere of mission is a world hostile to Jesus – behind those locked doors. The instrument of mission is the church of Jesus – joyful with the risen Lord in our midst. The divine agent of mission is the Holy Spirit of Jesus. He empowers us and convicts the world. The message of mission is the forgiveness of sins through Jesus – declared in the gospel. The method of mission is Scripture as testimony to Jesus – so that the blessing may come to those who have not seen and yet believed.

And so we see how the themes of our first four days coalesce. The forgiveness of sins is placarded by John the Baptist: 'Behold, the Lamb of God!' It is the reason we must 'feed' on Jesus' broken body and outpoured blood. The Holy Spirit convicts of sin that we may repent and confess our sins. The gift of the Holy Spirit is placarded by John the Baptist, taught by Jesus and finally poured out after the cross. The words of Jesus find their fulfilment in the apostolic testimony that becomes the New Testament.

And so, at the heart of our sending, there must always be human sinfulness, the cross of Jesus, the promise of the Spirit and the critical role of the Bible. Whatever else we do, let us be part of a church sent to speak from the Bible about the forgiveness of sins through the cross of Christ and the gift of the Spirit to all believers. For that will bring new life to men and women and be the deepest blessing we can bring to a world in great need.

Note

1. John Berridge, Bedfordshire minister in 1786, quoted in J. C. Ryle, *Five Christian Leaders* (Banner of Truth, 1960), p. 139.

The Lecture

Sent to the Front Line
Leadership in a Complex World

Richard Dannatt

Richard Dannatt was a soldier for forty years, concluding his military career as Chief of the General Staff – the professional head of the British Army. After retiring from active duty in 2009, he was Constable of the Tower of London until July 2016. In 2011 he became an independent member of the House of Lords. He was the founder Chairman of the Strategic Advisory Board of the Durham Global Security Institute, which focuses on conflict prevention through the integration of defence, diplomacy and development. He published his autobiography *Leading from the Front* in 2010 and a second book, *Boots on the Ground: Britain and Her Army since 1945*, in October 2016.

Sent to the Front Line
Leadership in a Complex World

Within the context of this morning's theme, 'Sent to the frontline', I had forty years on and off the frontline. These years divided fairly naturally into four decades, each of which had a very different characteristic. My first decade, the 1970s, was dominated by my service in Northern Ireland. My second decade, the 1980s, was the last decade of the Cold War. My third decade, the 1990s, began with the dust, if you like, of the Berlin Wall falling, but we quickly found ourselves in the dust of the Kuwaiti desert after Saddam Hussain had invaded Kuwait. However, that new world order didn't last long, taking the British Army into Bosnia and Kosovo. I'm often asked, 'Of your forty years in the army, which was the most satisfying period?' And I just paused when I mentioned Bosnia, because I was Commander of British Forces in 1995–1996 at the end of that ghastly civil war. And it was a great privilege to be part of the process that brought that war to a conclusion, managed the ceasefire process and began the process of implementing the peace agreement on the ground. My fourth decade in the army began with the attacks in New York and Washington, on 9/11, and propelled the British Army back into Iraq and Afghanistan. And in the decade since I left the army, it seems to me that our world has become even more complex, whether it's financial complexity, political complexity, Brexit complexity, or social complexity.

It's within this complex environment that I think there is a growing need for leadership as people and communities struggle to make sense of the world around them and ask: 'What do we do now?' So let me offer some views, purely from a personal perspective, on the leadership challenge generally. I first came across leadership as a subject to be considered formally while I was a cadet at the Royal Military Academy Sandhurst, where all British Army officers carry out their initial training. There leadership was not taught sitting in ranks in classrooms, but informally in armchairs, in the company bar. We were asked for our ideas as opposed to being told what to do and what to think. And I believe that immediately set leadership apart. It's a personal thing, it's an individual thing, it's an intuitive thing.

But despite that, I don't go as far as to subscribe to the notion that leaders are born, not made. Yes, a bit of natural leadership ability helps, and a lot of natural leadership ability helps a lot. But I think if you have any leadership ability, then thinking about the subject, studying the subject, experimenting, modelling yourself on a leader you respect – all those things can really pay dividends. When we sat around in our armchairs at Sandhurst we had fairly erudite discussions, on the one hand listing the qualities of a leader, and on the other hand, debating the merits of more functional or technical approaches to leadership. I remember extensive discussion about the thoughts of one of the previous heads of the army, the late Field Marshal Lord Harding. He'd produced an impressive list of qualities to be exhibited by a good leader: absolute fitness, complete integrity, enduring courage, daring initiative and undaunted willpower. And to these he added three other prerequisites: knowledge, judgment and team spirit.

Now, you're probably thinking that's all good stuff from a soldier's perspective, certainly applicable in what I would call the battle-space, but I suggest probably also equally applicable in the business space and the community space and elsewhere. But as respected and useful as possession of a large number of key qualities is in itself, our discussions at Sandhurst addressed more functional models of leadership. At the time there was something called the action-centred leadership model. It was illustrated by a classic Venn diagram of three interlocking and overlapping balls. And the model required three things: identify the task to be achieved; maximize the efforts of the team who are working with you; and look after the interests of the individual members of that team. I think that simple construct of task, team and individual, all working together, retains great merit. But one wonders, is that enough? I think what roots the discussion rather more is to analyse what the leader is actually trying to do. And to answer that, there's a need to have an understanding of what level of activity the leader is trying to lead within, and at which level he or she is trying to lead.

In my former sphere of work in the army, we separate out activity into three levels: the strategic, the operational and the tactical. I think in any field of work, the first and the last of those are well known. The strategic level is where the big thoughts are thought, and every business endeavour or large organization or even church group seems to be well supplied with strategic thought. And then down below, the tactical level is about delivery, getting it done. But as far as I'm concerned, the key level of activity is the operational level, the level which sits between the strategic and the tactical. In fact it's the level which turns the ideas *into* action, and in my book that's the level which lifts the mediocre to the exceptional. It's the level that lifts, if you like, Nelson, Wellington and Montgomery into the history books, and the like of Bill Gates and Richard Branson into the world's rich lists. Because it's at this operational level where the general, captain of industry, or the boss, does his or her real work, and where an end-to-end plan is formulated to transform the original idea, the big idea, into success on the battlefield, profit on the balance sheet, or success in the community project.

You might think that the case that I'm making is all very well, in sorting out the strategic from the operational, to the tactical, in a large enterprise like an army or a big multinational company. But where is the application in a small business, a charity, a church, or even in a community project? Well I would suggest that in any application, size in itself doesn't matter. Even in a small business or small enterprise there will always be moments when a strategic review will be needed. And yes, there will always be moments, probably a majority of the time, when leading the workforce at the tactical level, getting the people on the journey with you, will be essential. But most critically, there really must be those moments when you are engaged in what I have called this 'operational level thought', to work out the campaign plan which translates the strategic objectives into tactical, practical success. Be it a positive outcome on the battlefield, or success in any community enterprise. Whether in a large or a small enterprise, what's really critical is weaving together those three levels of activity.

But then the question is how to do all this? In the organization in which I grew up we exercise leadership through a process known as 'mission command', and we aim to do this in both day-to-day life and on operations. But I would apply the principle more widely still. It's a plea for decentralization; it's a plea to let decisions be taken at their most appropriate level. Essentially there are three components to what we call mission command and they all hinge around the leader. First the leader needs to think through the situation, his challenge and his problem, and convert his strategic goals into the front end of his operational campaign plan. This then results in him clearly setting out his intent in a short, concise statement. He needs to have applied sufficient analysis and intellectual rigour so he can set out to his subordinates or his employees, his statement of what needs to be done and his statement of his overall intentions as to how it's to be done. And I suggest that it's more than just a rather wishy-washy vision statement on the company office wall. This is personal leadership business, and not a corporate staff activity.

The second stage, in a non-prescriptive way, is to separate out the tasks that need to be done and then to delegate them to more junior team leaders or individuals, along with the necessary manpower, equipment and money to carry out those tasks. But the boss doesn't tell them what to do. He tells them what to achieve. So this is very much output or outcome focused, not input focused. It is harnessing their initiative. Finally, and this is where the process can go wrong, having delegated the tasks in a reasonable fashion, he or she needs to supervise the execution of those tasks appropriately. This is achieved not in a way that stifles that initiative of those to whom the tasks have been delegated, but in a subtle and nuanced way, while always remembering that while tasks can be delegated, responsibility can never be delegated. The buck always stops with the boss. He or she owns the overall plan.

Changing tack a little, a leader does indeed need certain qualities, of which integrity is key. At the same time, there are certain capabilities that a leader needs as well – to understand the objectives, to map out this route from strategic end-state to tactical decisions, above all communicating the intent clearly, delegating responsibly, but critically remembering he can never delegate responsibility. But I wonder whether these qualities and capabilities that I've suggested are enough. Fitness, integrity, courage, initiative, willpower: these things and more are really important. But are they enough? As an organization the British Army thought not. After much discussion we identified six core values which have become the heart of the ethos of the army: selfless commitment, courage, discipline, integrity, loyalty and respect for others. Are they themselves enough? My own feeling is that a range of leadership qualities and these core values provide a very sound moral baseline that's acceptable to all, albeit quite a challenge to live up to.

But is a sound moral baseline enough? Should there not also be a spiritual dimension to this? Perhaps unsurprisingly, I believe there should be. Of course, it's that word 'believe' or 'belief' that is at the heart of any spiritual dimension. For some, belief in the cause, the leader, or – in the army – belief in the strength of the regiment, will be enough. But what really sustains, in my view, is something more than this, something far bigger and deeper than we can imagine or rationalize for ourselves. This first came home to me, as a platoon commander in Northern Ireland in the early 1970s, when my platoon got caught up in a particularly fierce gunfight in Belfast. Bullets flew up and down the street in a rather alarming way. At the end of the day we had killed at least two terrorists and wounded a number of others. Two of my soldiers had been shot, one of whom tragically died of his wounds shortly afterwards. Whatever anyone said later that day, everybody had been scared witless. But that experience told me that even the toughest of men, when the chips are down and the reality of life and death confronts, are reaching out into the spiritual dimension, beyond the rational and beyond the moral. I don't think this just applies to armies in a combat situation. I think there's a direct application to any situation of pressure, stress or challenge when individuals are stretched to their physical or psychological limits. After all, where do you go to when you've lost your job? Or your firm has gone bust?

I think the truly effective leader needs to recognize this question. But he or she is of course personally challenged to provide what is needed, to provide the response. And if the leader doesn't have some empathy with, or some experience of a spiritual dimension within their own lives, then where does the leader go to provide that strength and guidance to those for whom he or she is responsible? When the face is turned to the leader, with the unspoken question, 'What do we do now?' into what reserve does the leader go for his or her inspiration? But I stress that this is a personal thing, and something that any leader has got to work out for ourselves. But work it out we must, because people will look to the boss for leadership in this area, as much, if not more, than other areas.

But any of us in these difficult circumstances should remember that we are not the first to have trodden this path. One aspect of leadership development, accepting that others may have trod where we now step, is the identification and deliberate modelling that you really respect as a leader. In my experience, a number of people left a lasting impression on me. But if we're lifting the discussion to a spiritual dimension, then there is one obvious role model to look at: the person and example of Christ. Christians, quite rightly, put a huge emphasis on the death and resurrection of Christ, but his life also provides the model that I believe leaders will do well to try to emulate. The motto of the Royal Military Academy Sandhurst is, 'Serve to lead'. Christ in his lifetime is a very clear example of that maxim. When Christ washed his disciples' feet, he was doing the most menial and humble task. And by serving his disciples, he was earning the right to lead them. He would ask of others nothing he would not do himself. And his style of leadership? It was to say quite simply: 'Follow me.' It was not said in a macho way but in a way that gave people the opportunity to look at him – what he stood for, what he promised – and to decide for themselves whether to follow him or not. This is key: the flipside of leadership is followership, and the trick of being a successful leader is to encourage people to choose freely to follow, not out of curiosity, but out of belief and confidence that the direction of travel is right and the objective is worth the costs along the way.

Following his Father's plan cost Jesus Christ his life. But his belief and confidence in his Father's plan led to him opening up the way to peace and purpose in this life and life beyond, for those who are also prepared to put their trust in him. In my former business, asking people to risk their lives is part of the job. But doing so without giving them the chance to understand the meaning of life and death, I believe, is something of a dereliction of our wider duty of care to our people. And therefore I think there is very much an obligation on the leader, certainly on the Christian leader, to include a spiritual dimension into his people's general conduct for their lives, and in my case, their preparation for potentially life-challenging operations. Qualities and core values are fine as a universally acceptable moral baseline for leadership. But the unique life, death, resurrection and promises of Christ provide that spiritual opportunity that I believe takes the privilege and demand of leadership to another level.

Next, the leader needs also to exercise great clarity in explaining to others what needs to be done, something that's particularly critical in the complex times in which we live. Fortunately, in the Christian context, we have an example of the issuing of orders for battle by none other than St Paul himself. When Paul wrote about putting on the whole armour of God in Ephesians 6, there was a real battle to be fought for the hearts of men and women, a battle between good and evil, what is right and what is wrong. It was so in his day, and it is in ours. And so he gave very clear orders for battle and they're worth looking at in just a little more detail.

Now, anyone here with a military background will know that the template for the successful passage of orders to initiate an operation or campaign is to follow this sequence explaining the situation, giving the mission, detailing the method of execution, describing the administration or logistics necessary, and then concluding via the command arrangements. And this is exactly what St Paul does. He sets us a very good leadership example. In Ephesians 6:12, he wrote: 'We are not contending against flesh and blood, but against the principalities, against the powers, against the world rulers of this present darkness, against the spiritual hosts of wickedness in the heavenly places' (RSV). First, Paul was describing the complex world of his day, and from that description there is no doubt that the situation was grim. It was grim for Christ at Calvary, it was grim in Paul's day and it remains grim in our day. The enemy, if you like, is all around us, whether it's downright opposition to the Christian faith or the more insidious erosion of the Christian basis of our country through misunderstood multiculturalism and supposed political correctness.

Second, we get our mission in verse 11, 'stand against the wiles of the devil' and in case we have missed it, it's repeated in verse 14, 'stand therefore' (RSV). This is an unequivocal mission. We stand for what is good, right and true. We stand on and for the promises of almighty God. Third, it gets even more exciting as we're told how to do this. Put on the 'whole armour of God', Paul says, and the physical and spiritual components of that armour for offensive and defensive operations are listed for us. We know them well so I won't dwell on them, other than to comment that without a belt a soldier cannot carry his equipment. Paul is talking about the belt of truth, and truth can often be the first casualty of war. But with this belt of truth we have the confidence that what he has said and read about almighty God is indeed true. The breastplate of righteousness is a soldier's character and integrity. Can we trust our leaders? Do our soldiers trust us? We can place our complete trust in Christ. Nothing will get through that breastplate. And the feet are properly shod and protected for the difficult task of taking the gospel of peace far and wide to wherever we're sent on the frontline. The shield of faith should be so strong that it can withstand the critical attacks of our opponents, and absorb our own doubts when things happen that we fail to understand. Moreover, the helmet protects our head, our capacity to think, which, when linked to our heart, provides the capacity to inspire. So these things – the belt, the breastplate, the boots, the shield and the helmet – are the items of equipment needed for defensive operations to ensure that we can stand firm as Christians.

The last item mentioned is the vital bit of equipment for offensive operations: 'the sword of the Spirit, which is the word of God'. It is the Word of God that can change lives, communities and nations. As a young officer I got into the habit of carrying a very small New Testament with me. It's rather battered now, but years ago I wrote inside the front cover: 'This little book is always carried inside my combat jacket pocket. It's a symbol of that great love that is more powerful than any force of evil, and is the source of light, comfort and hope in situations of darkness, misery and despair.' And on the facing page I've progressively added the names and dates of my operational tours. That page is fairly full now. But inside the back cover, I wrote out some other very familiar words: 'I will lift up mine eyes to the hills from whence cometh my help. My help cometh from the Lord which made the heaven and the earth' (KJV). There is no question of us invoking God to be on our side in a conflict, whether a secular or a spiritual one. But we need to be on God's side, as it was he who made the heavens and earth, and he is the source of our help. But back to Paul's template for orders for battle.

The next section *should* be about administration and logistics, but like many commanders in a hurry he seems to have overlooked that. We'll pass over that omission in a generous way, but in order to placate any logisticians among you, a general's ambition, his ambitious operation designs, must rightly be enabled or constrained by the art of what is logistically possible. But Paul has much to say about the final section – command and control. In verse 18 he writes, 'pray in the Spirit on all occasions, with all kinds of prayers and requests'. Even on the modern hi-tech battlefield, communications can break down between a commander and his troops. But with God, our communications can never fail. We have direct access to the commander-in-chief at any time and on any matter,

and this is a huge advantage that we forget at our peril. And
finally, Paul knew that we are at our most vulnerable when
we drop our guard and can be surprised. His final words
in these orders for battle therefore are 'be alert'.

If the Christian leader is now fully equipped for defensive
and offensive operations, I would say that we also need
a personal design for battle – a concept for operations, a
framework for one's own life to focus our actions in the
complex circumstances around us. I suggest we need to
embrace three things, and they're potentially life-changing.
We need to ask ourselves whether we are prepared to be
obedient to God, committed to Christ, and open to the
Holy Spirit.

As an example of obedience to God, consider the story
of the Old Testament warrior Gideon (Judges 6 – 8). On
God's instructions he endorsed an amazing concept of
operations. He reduced his troops from 22,000 to 300.
Deploying his tiny force at night – a force equipped more
like the regimental band than crack troops – the result was
that 135,000 were defeated. This was an astonishing victory,
stemming from obedience to God, and of course I could
quote many other examples. But listening to God and
doing what he prompts us to do is the baseline. What
Christ wants from us is full commitment and not a half-
hearted compromise. It was not until, as a 26-year-old
captain, I had a major stroke, that I really considered the
quality of my commitment to Christ. The day was
11 November 1977, the anniversary of Armistice Day,
when at the eleventh hour of the eleventh day of the

eleventh month of 1918, the surrender of Germany to end the First World War was announced. But a surrender is two things: it's the end of the fighting and the beginning of the peace. I found, after years of fighting with my Creator, compromising and ignoring his challenges, that a far better way of life was to commit myself wholeheartedly to him, to surrender my will to his will and thereby gain the peace and purpose in life that only complete trust in Jesus Christ can give.

But obedience and commitment are not enough, I would suggest, unless transformed by the enabling power of the Holy Spirit. One of my favourite passages in the Bible is the closing verses of John 14. Verses 25–26 says: 'These things I have spoken to you, while I am still with you. But the Counselor, the Holy Spirit, whom the Father will send in my name, he will teach you all things, and bring to your remembrance all that I have said to you' (RSV). Jesus is saying that the Father will send the Spirit to those who are obedient to God, committed to Christ, and prepared to be open to the Holy Spirit, because the Father wants us to use the abilities that we've been given to work to bring peace and enrichment to the lives of individuals. Whether we're doing so as a leader at the strategic level, or as a fighter at the tactical level, wherever we are sent on the frontline, the Holy Spirit will guide, direct and inspire us, if only we are open to him.

If we can construct a picture of these three aspects – obedience to God, commitment to Christ and openness to the Holy Spirit – as another of those three-ball Venn diagrams, the centre section of that diagram is still missing. I firmly believe that the focus that makes sense of all this is the cross of Christ. To be truly effective as a leader or as a foot soldier, the cross must be at the centre of our lives, because kneeling at the foot of Christ's cross is the recruiting office where our spiritual journey and our duty begins. This is where our spiritual pilgrimage is focused, and where the real challenge and spiritual warfare begins in this complex world. Jesus lived as the perfect man, died on the cross, taking the weight of our sin on his shoulders, but he rose again, breaking the power of sin and death and guilt, and in doing so he charted the everlasting path to peace. It's my experience that an encounter with the person of Jesus Christ at the cross changes lives. It can change individuals and it can have a strategic effect not only *on* individuals but *through* individuals. The cross brings God's peace to those who are prepared to meet Christ on the cross and to surrender their lives to him and say, 'not my will but thy will for my life'. Moreover, it's my experience that a life which is obedient to God, committed to Christ and open to the Holy Spirit sustains and guides in these complex times. But there is no getting away from it: leading such a life comes at a cost. Remember Christ's words in Mark 8:34, 'If any man would come after me, let him deny himself and take up his cross and follow me' (RSV). There is no doubt that there is a cost to following Christ today. Such a path is counter-cultural to many in our increasingly secular society. But if that cost seems daunting as we go forward to the frontline as leaders and soldiers in this complex world, then it's worth remembering too the promise of God in Revelation 2:10, 'Be thou faithful unto death, and I will give thee a crown of life' (KJV).

The Seminar

Empowering and Engaging Our Seniors

Louise Morse

Louise Morse is a cognitive behavioural therapist, confer-
ence speaker, broadcaster and researcher. She works for
the Pilgrims' Friend Society and is the author of several
books on old age, including dementia. This seminar is
based on her latest book, *What's Age Got to Do with It?*

Empowering and Engaging Our Seniors

What do we mean by 'old'? I guarantee you think it's ten years older than you are! And how old do you feel inside? Does anybody feel old inside? Most of you feel young. But when you look in the mirror, what do you see? They say you know you're growing old when you look in the mirror and your mother's face looks back at you. But when you think about how you feel inside and what you view on the outside, isn't that an example of what the apostle Paul wrote about? We are spiritual beings in earthly vessels (2 Corinthians 5). This earthly tent is decaying, but the real us that will live for ever is being transformed from one degree of glory to another (2 Corinthians 3:18). What I'd like to see at the end of this seminar is a changed perception, on the part of all of us, on what it means to be old. God created old age on purpose, and seniors have roles that God designed *on purpose* for age, experience and wisdom.

The Bible espouses a wisdom-based society and, generally speaking, wisdom comes as you age? We learn from our experiences, don't we? Who couldn't say that you wish you'd known at twenty what you know now. Knowledge is not the same as wisdom. You could get an older person who isn't wise. But if that older person is a Christian, that will tell you they haven't been walking very closely with the Lord, because you know how the Holy Spirit nudges you until you do the right thing. Old age was intended from God to be a blessing and a gift. Biblical wisdom says, 'With long life I will satisfy him and show him my salvation' (Psalm 91:16). 'Do not forget my teaching, but keep my commands in your heart, for they will prolong your life' (Proverbs 3:1–2).

Lifetimes have been extending for the past thirty years, and there is no sign of that stopping. Most people don't realize that the incidence of dementia – that is, the new cases of people in their sixties, seventies, and early eighties, being diagnosed – is actually falling. It's fallen by 20% over the past twenty years, for the same reason that we're living longer – because we're living better lifestyles. We've stopped smoking, we're eating better, and we're beginning to take exercise. Above all, education is improving, and one of the secrets of a good, healthy brain (at any age, but especially old age), is to keep on using it. It is true, you either use it or lose it.

The Bible reflects a society where wisdom was exalted. When Paul was writing to Philemon, someone who had come to faith through him, Paul appealed to him to show mercy to his runaway servant, Onesimus, saying, 'Paul, the aged' (NKJV). He wasn't saying 'I, Paul, the decrepit, crawling along.' No, he said, 'I, Paul, the senior one, am appealing to you not just because of what I've done for you in leading you to the Lord, but because I am a senior.' Wisdom of seniors was acknowledged, and it was *enabled* by that acknowledgement.

So what did God design old age for? Well, Christians in old age are the proof of the pudding, aren't they? Think about it: a Christian can stand at the age of eighty and say, 'God has always been there for me, he has never let me down.' Of course, nobody has a perfect life. I believe that we should teach our children and our grandchildren that life is tough. Life is not fair, it is impacted by the fall. But older people have been through the deep waters, they've been through the fire, and they can say, 'God was with me.' 'Since my youth, God, you have taught me, and to this day I declare your marvellous deeds' (Psalm 71:17).

Our seniors, then, are to teach and encourage the younger generation. We see this in Paul's writing to Titus and Timothy. Seniors are to mentor, to listen to and strengthen society, to be an unofficial but recognized elderhood. Think about the Sherpas who guide people up Everest. People who go up the mountain without guides tend not to do very well, do they? But Sherpas are guides, and that's in a sense what old people are. A very eminent secular psychologist summed it up very well when he said, 'Let's entertain the idea that character requires the additional years and that the long-lasted life is forced upon us neither by genes, nor by conservation or medicine, nor by societal collusion. I have yet to see societal collusion engender old age.' That's what he said. The last years of life conform and fulfil character.

Generally it's agreed that older people have more patience, wisdom, and empathy. There's a famous experiment to test reactions, in which younger people and older people were fed very negative views about themselves. 'He looks sneaky'; 'she's impatient'; 'she looks very critical'; 'I wouldn't trust someone with a face like that' – that sort of thing. The younger ones were very annoyed, and they wanted to know who wrote those things, they wanted to speak to them. The older ones said, 'Ah well, everybody's got their own views, haven't they?' You see, you reach a stage of emotional equilibrium. You reach a stage where you're able to take the long view because you've experienced something similar, and you know God works things out. This is not to say that older people are sin-free. I have a friend who's a very keen theologian and he says that there are sins that are peculiar to old age. We disagree about this. He says older people can be impatient, over-indulgent and full of self-pity. But actually, as a cognitive behavioural therapist, I think these are things you have *in you* at any age. It's just that when you're older, you don't have the energy to restrain them. So if you've been a grumpy young lady, you're going to be a grumpy old lady!

To sum up so far, I've explained that God intended old age for his specific purposes so that we, living with him through life's experiences, would develop the attributes we need to be the glue that holds society together. But before we come into all that God intended us to be, we must tackle ageism. It's widespread. Age UK says that nearly a million people feel their lives have no meaning because they're old. They believe the myth that because you are old your brain will inevitably slow down. That is not true. Some peoples' brains slow down. A lot of the frailty of old age – unless you get hit by the proverbial bus, have an inherited disease, or develop a severe illness – is related to disuse syndrome. We don't move enough. Researchers recently showed that we develop new neurons – it's called neurogenesis, operating in our brains until we die. It was thought until quite recently that as you aged, your brain stopped making new neurons, neuronal circuits, but that's not the case at all. We go on developing new circuits as we use our brains until we die. The man who, at the age of fifty-six, revolutionized mobile phones by inventing the lithium battery patented another battery that will revolutionize electric cars last year, at the age of ninety-four. The 105-year-old who is still teaching yoga, the 101-year-old who expanded her business by buying another sewing machine, are thought to be exceptions, but they're not. It's just we don't hear these stories because the press is mainly generated by younger people.

So many churches report their over-fifties are slipping away. After a talk I gave in Cardiff a pastor said, 'Can you tell me how to keep my older members engaged?' The first question that came into my mind was: 'What responsibility are you giving them? What do they feel in charge of? What do they feel a part of?' I was in a church recently where a pastor announced that they were having a big push to attract younger people and he said, 'And you older people, you'll have to move out of your comfort zone.' He had categorized young and old. I haven't had the chance to ask him, 'Why did you say that? Why didn't you say, "You older people, I want your heart in this, I want your ideas in this."' We all want more young people in our churches, don't we? But we've categorized young and old, and that creates ageism, because when you create a category in society like that, what you're saying is 'us' and 'them', and 'them' can become objects. It's hard to have empathy with objects. We have empathy with people like us, don't we?

Ageism manifests as a lot of things. W. H. Thomas, who wrote the book *What Are Old People for?*, talks about the virulent ageism that we've seen since the war. Before the war we didn't have adolescence and teenage angst, did we? We didn't have this emphasis on youth. Being young was not the peak of our society's ambition. You weren't urged to stay young and beautiful, were you? He thinks this ageism is because of the influence of the Baby Boomers. The Baby Boomer generation influenced the culture of every decade that it went through. Some of you will remember the riots of 1969–70. They changed our culture. Traditional views were thrown out of the window and unfortunately it coincided with the contraceptive pill, which meant that even more values, the things that held us together, were weakened.

The Baby Boomers influenced our society radically, because their life-design concept was that first you were young and then you grew to be a teenager. You were starting to be somebody when you were a teenager and then you became an adult. As a productive, economy-driving adult, you were a master of the universe. Their design concept meant that, when you were old, you simply hurtled into an abyss of brokenness. To be old was not to be where it's at. The word 'ageism' was coined by Dr Rob Butler in 1969, and he described perfectly the manufactured intergenerational warfare that we're seeing today.

This was brought home to me recently when I bought a new iron. I took it out of the box and I was dumbfounded because it had more controls than my car! I thought, 'I'll have to ask my grandson how to use this.' My grandson is nineteen and he was born with technology in his brain. I looked at my new iron and I thought of my grandma's iron. My grandma had one of those little black irons. Do you remember them? It was hot or it wasn't, and she used to spit on it to see if it was working! This generation has absorbed more technology than any other generation in history, and yet older people are still being portrayed as thick! As a cognitive behavioural therapist I want to ask: 'Where is the evidence for that?' Sometimes feelings are so strong that we have what's known as a cognitive distortion; in other words, we believe our feelings and not the facts. This iron was a real eye-opener to me. Older people are not necessarily slow. Sometimes a really old person can be slower overall, because they have a cardio-vascular insufficiency – their circulation isn't what it was. Again, it points to the importance of moving in old age. The thing is, we get very efficient as we get older, don't we? We'll put something on the bottom step of the stairs, and then we'll wait until we have other things to take up. But actually what we should do is take it upstairs straight away. (As a vicar said to a friend of mine, 'Do you ever think of the hereafter?' 'Yes,' she said, 'every time I go upstairs, I think "What am I here after?"')

So how do we engage and empower seniors for the role God intended? Often when you step down from a job that you've done particularly well, you sense that you don't have a role. Ephesians 2:10 tells you that that isn't true. God has a purpose for us, and that's what I want everybody over the age of sixty to go away with. And you don't have to worry about finding your good works, because 'A man's heart plans his way, but the LORD directs his steps' (Proverbs 16:9 NKJV). God will bring your good works to you. We need to examine what we mean by good works as well. What's really important in God's economy? It's not often the same thing that we think is important in our lives. In God's economy, building one another up is so important. I constantly look for ways of building a person up because I have a natural Welsh inclination to be critical. When I'm sitting on the underground, going to my office, I look at people and I say, 'God, who needs you here today?' And I'll pray for them – in my head! When you walk down a street and see a homeless person or a youngster who's not well cared for, don't let them just walk past – pray for them. You might be the only person who's prayed for them. Stay close to God so you can see what he wants you to do. It's so powerful to pray, but there are other things too: serving tea in church with a smile, that's good; but more important is having a say in all the key decisions that your church makes. 'We are [God's] workmanship, created in Christ Jesus for good works which God prepared beforehand that we should walk in them' (Ephesians 2:10, NKJV). Psalm 139:16 says, 'All the days ordained for me were written in your book before one of them came to be.' Isn't that amazing? Psalm 138:8, 'The LORD will accomplish what concerns me' (NASB).

Let me give you some examples of people who are un-affected by ageism and how much they achieve. David Chapman was ninety-five and living in a Christian care home in South Wales. Because the home took non-Christians he wanted Christian support – people who would pray for the staff, befriend residents, lead services. He emailed sixty evangelical churches in his area and arranged a day to launch a befriending scheme for his home. I think thirty churches attended and he signed people up as 'friends' of his particular home. David is now ninety-eight, he walks with the aid of a cane, but inside he is on fire for the Lord. He wants those who are not Christians in his care home to know the Lord. He's not in a position to preach to them, and that wouldn't work anyway. But these evangelical supporters who have come in are showing kindness, they're showing sacrifice, they're giving their time. The first thing they did was clear up the rose garden. Practical things!

Irene came into our Plymouth home. She was given three months to live but she actually lived for eighteen months. She was totally bed-ridden and needed everything done for her. She said to her friend, 'I feel so useless – I feel that I have no purpose.' So her friend, who was linked to a Romanian home for children, said, 'Why don't you learn to knit? You could knit blankets.' So she did. And her friend gave her photographs that she had taken of children using the blankets when she went to Romania. Then Irene decided to knit poppies for Poppy Day. You couldn't walk past her room without buying a poppy. She sold seventy pounds worth of poppies! She had a letter from the British Legion thanking her. She felt she had a purpose in still helping others. There are so many more examples. In one of the worst parts of Manchester, five evangelical churches are working together on a community outreach project. They have, at the last count, forty-six 'befrienders', nearly all older people. The police and social services send them referrals of people who are older and lonely. They befriend them, and they're all older people themselves. I interview people in their eighties and nineties who are still active: they don't look for things to do – things come to them. They say, 'Retire? Why would I want to retire?' You know, in the Bible, the only people who retired were the Levites. And they were encouraged to stay on and help their brethren, so they were able to share the wisdom they'd gained from their experience in serving, without having to do the heavy lifting.

But how can we actually change perception? The biggest way to change perception is to change behaviour. We feel we have to change attitudes first. If that were the case, you wouldn't get free samples from companies who pay millions of pounds a year to psychologists. The reason you get free samples is not to taste it and see that it's nice, it's to change your behaviour. Until you've changed your behaviour, you're not going to change your attitude towards their product, are you? So what I'd like to see is us recognizing the elderhood that God designed older people for, to preach from the pulpit on their value and purpose. Not, 'Older people, you have to move out of your comfort zone so we can reach the young.' But, 'Older people, I want your ideas for reaching the young.' Enable seniors to tell out God's faithfulness. Give them ten minutes on a Sunday to say: 'This is what God has done for me.' I heard of one man who gave a testimony of how he was one of the first to go into Belsen. He told what it was like, rolling up in the trucks and seeing the prisoners there in striped clothes. The younger ones in the congregation were spellbound. Also, search yourself: are you having ageist thoughts? Are you thinking, 'Oh what can I expect at my age?' Why?

> Grow old along with me!
> The best is yet to be,
> The last of life, for which the first was made:
> Our times are in His hand
> Who saith, 'A whole, I planned,
> Youth shows but half; trust God: see all, nor be afraid!
> (*Rabbi Ben Ezra* by Robert Browning)

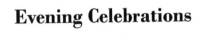

Evening Celebrations

God's Remedy

Christopher Chia

Christopher Chia was converted from a Buddhist-Taoist heritage at a Billy Graham Crusade. He is the Senior Pastor of Adam Road Presbyterian Church, a leading gospel-centred church in Singapore and South-East Asia. Chris has been blessed with an international ministry of preaching and being a pastor to pastors. He loves nature walks, dogs, music, movies, his wife and his two adult children, but not necessarily in that order.

God's Remedy
Isaiah 42:1–9

I do not know whether you've ever watched the programme *Kids Say the Darnedest Things*. In this particular
programme, the interviewers were asking children for
their views on the greatest problems in the world and the
solutions to these problems. And so the first child said
the greatest problem in the world is pollution. 'Pollution?'
asked the interviewer. 'What would be the solution to
this?' The three Rs: renew, reuse and repeat. The second
child said, 'The greatest problem in the world is nuclear
weapons', and answered that the solution is to get rid
of nuclear weapons. Finally another child put up a hand
and the interviewer asked, 'So from your perspective
what's the greatest problem in the world?' This child
replied: 'My younger brother.' And the solution? 'Get rid
of him!'

Sometimes our experiences of problems and solutions are light-hearted and humorous. My parents came from China in the early 1900s and they settled in Malaya, which became Malaysia, Singapore. My father had a sister, and she married a man who turned out to be a womanizer. He actually died of a sexually transmitted disease. It traumatized my auntie and she became mentally unsound. When my father heard about this he travelled to where his sister had settled. She had become a beggar. She had become so destitute that she would eat at the food centres, and whatever leftover food there was, she would just gobble it up. So my father took his sister home. She lived at the back of our house and we looked after her till her dying days. And every so often, when we were late in giving her lunch or dinner, she would burst into our house and grab whatever food was on the table and smear it on her face. My father would be both ashamed and angry at the same time. And once or twice, as a young boy, I saw my dad standing at the window just staring out. Everything within him loved his sister. Everything within him wanted to help his sister. But nothing could help her because she was mentally unsound from her traumatic marriage. Sometimes our experience of problems and solutions are not light-hearted like *Kids Say the Darnedest Things* – they are heavy-hearted. The bigger the problem, the better the solution has to be. The more life-threatening the problem, the more life-saving the solution has to be.

The book of Isaiah begins with a problem: it's the biggest and the most life-threatening problem. It is God exposing and judging his people Judah and his city, Jerusalem, for failing him, for two-timing him. And so I'm going to spend the first ten minutes just drawing the big picture of the book of Isaiah for you. One way to cheat at this is to read the first and last chapters of the book. Isaiah begins with a rotten Jerusalem and ends with a renewed Jerusalem. Why do I say that it begins with a spiritually rotten and morally decadent Jerusalem and people? If you walk quickly through chapter 1, what is the picture you get? Israel is experiencing spiritual rot, economic rot, and injustice. It is in spiritual and moral decay. No love for neighbour, foreigner, the fatherless or the widow. It sounds like Washington, London, Singapore! This shouldn't ever sound like Jerusalem, the city of God. But Jerusalem is comprehensively, thoroughly, totally rotten – a million miles away from God. And so she faces a personal, individual, national, global and cosmic problem because God's purposes began all those years ago with a promise to Abraham to bless, bless, bless (Genesis 12:1–3). All those blessings find their channel and their vessel in Jerusalem and the people of Jerusalem. But Jerusalem was no longer a symbol of the truth and light, no longer a city that drew nations to the true and living God. That's how the book begins. Let's take a snapshot of how it ends.

> For behold, I create new heavens
>> and a new earth,
> and the former things shall not be remembered
>> or come to mind.

But be glad and rejoice for ever
   in that which I create;
for behold, I create Jerusalem to be a joy,
   and her people to be a gladness.
(65:17–18, ESV)

This is a new and renewed, recreated Jerusalem. The book
has moved from failed worship in chapter 1 to the global
city of worship, not simply for the Jews and the Israelites,
but for all nations. How does Jerusalem go from a spiritual
pariah, as it were, to the spiritual poster boy? From being
an inglorious city of God to the glorious city of God?
The instrument and the key is the person and work of the
Servant of the Lord. And that is why Isaiah 40 – 55 is
the fulcrum, the watershed, the key, for it is through the
Servant of the Lord that God himself takes it from a rotten,
decadent city to be the glorious city of God where all
nations will stream in. So with that backdrop we can now
plunge into Isaiah 42.

This passage of nine verses can be divided very simply
into two portions. In verses 1–4, the Lord speaks of his
Servant, describing the task of the Servant. From verses
5–9, the Lord speaks to his Servant, affirming the task of
his Servant. The Servant is the key to the personal, national
and global worship of God. In Isaiah 42, the identity of the
Servant is not so much the key, as is the task of the Servant.
And it begins, verse 1: 'Behold my servant' (ESV) or in some
versions, 'Look'. In Isaiah 41:29, we are told, 'look' at the
idolaters. And now in Isaiah 42, 'Look at my servant.' Be

careful where you look. The people of Israel were so dazzled by the idolatry of all the pagan nations they found themselves in that they no longer looked to God by looking to his Word or his covenant. They look in the wrong direction. And the only one that could rescue them from this addictive idolatry, from this addictive adultery against God, was the Servant of the Lord. So be careful where you look, my friends.

I'm an unusual Chinaman. I love dogs. I don't eat dogs. Once we had a golden retriever and I thought I'd trained it to quite a high standard of obedience to walk and run beside me hands-free. So I took it out for a walk. In Singapore there is a reservoir with a zig-zag bridge across it. It's quite pretty, built by the British – must be nice! And I remember running on the zig-zag bridge, my dog running beside me on a lead. I put the lead on my belt hook on my shorts. I turned right and my dog turned left, and my zipper burst. And my shorts came down to my knees! I could see the headline in my head: 'Pastor caught streaking in park!' To this day, I have no idea what distracted my dog – was it a monkey, a cat, a dog? I thought it was quite well trained and it kept its eyes on me, but you know, disobedience – primal disobedience – runs deep. I thought it was loyal to me, but the moment it saw a distraction, it turned the other way! Be careful where you look, my friends. In our fallen sinful nature, we are prone to give our love, our loyalty, our life to idols and not to God. And that was the trouble Israel got herself into. She looked and listened to the wrong people. So the Servant will come to turn the gaze of God's people to the rightful person they should gaze upon.

What do we know about this Servant? Verse 1, 'uphold' – literally means 'I grip'. There are many servants in the Old Testament, from Moses to David and everyone in between. But this Servant is God's Servant par excellence. He is without measure, without comparison. This is *the* Servant, not *a* Servant. And 'my soul delights' (ESV). You know you can be chosen for a team but you still may not be the apple of the coach's eye. The Servant is the apple of God's eye and he will get the permanent and powerful presence of God's Spirit: 'I will put my Spirit upon him.' This is totally different from all the servants of the Old Testament who got the presence of God's Spirit temporarily. Here is the Servant that gets the permanent presence of the Spirit. And the Servant's task? He accomplishes justice. Three times the word 'justice' is used. Justice could mean the 'micro-justice', when you and I do wrong to each other as neighbours. But it could also be referring to what I call 'macro-justice'. In Isaiah 41 there is a court case going on between God and the idols. God is winning this case and the justice, the 'macro-justice', is to give God his due. God's Servant steps on to the world stage to give God his due – his praise, his worship, as the centre of the universe. No other servant will accomplish this task, but the Servant of the Lord will put the God of the universe at its centre.

What else do we know about the attitude of this Servant? Verse 2, 'He will not shout or cry out' – he is self-effacing, self-forgetting. 'A bruised reed he will not break, and a smouldering wick he will not snuff out' (verse 3). You look at a bruised reed and say, 'Oh that's useless, I'm not going to take it home!' A smouldering wick – a candle that's going out – it's too far gone. But for this Servant, nothing is in the 'too hard to do' basket. As for himself, verse 4, 'he will not falter'. The Hebrew word is the same as verse 3 – he himself will not burn low like a smouldering wick. He will not be discouraged. There is much we do not know about this Servant, but his posture, his attitude, is totally meek and vulnerable. But, friends, we know the gospel story. There is invincibility in the Servant's vulnerability. Please do not reach the premature and mistaken conclusion that just because he is meek, he is weak; that just because he's vulnerable, he'll never be victorious. The Servant of the Lord, who comes to put God at centre-stage, will display his invincibility through his vulnerabilities.

From verses 5 to 9, the Lord speaks to his Servant, affirming his task. Just in case you do not remember, *Yahweh* – the name of God given to Moses in Exodus 3 – is the creator and sustainer of all things, and therefore he should rightly get the glory from all (verse 5). How dare Israel give glory to idols? How dare Israel, Judah and Jerusalem steal glory for themselves? We arrived in the UK a few days ago and drove down to Land's End. It's glorious. As I was driving I noticed a Tesco food truck and it had this slogan, 'freshly clicked'. We have gone from a farming nation where we rejoice in freshly picked vegetables to a whole new generation of millennials and Gen Y or Z, who believe that food grows in the computer and in the phone. If you're ever hungry you just click. It's a brilliant slogan, but we are fast losing the awe of God! One of our church members climbed up one of the lower peaks near Mount Everest. He said to me, 'You know what I said when I got to that mountain peak? "I'm so small!"' You should get out there to creation and realize, 'I'm so small'. He is God and I am not. He is creator and I am creature. He is maker and I am made. Every so often, as we live in a world of idols and idolatry, of science and technology, we forget that. We forget our 'creatureliness'. Israel forgot that.

Now God speaks to the Servant. Verse 6, 'I will give you as a covenant for the people, a light for the nations' (ESV). The Servant is the embodiment of God's covenant. He is the residential address of God's covenant or contract with this people. In short, if you still don't get it, the Servant is God's final revelation, his final redemption, a light to the Gentiles. And the Servant comes and does three things: he opens blind eyes, frees the prisoners, and releases us from the dungeon of darkness. Historically this could refer to the Israelites being released from the bondage of exile. But finally, it is the release from the bondage of Satan, and death caused by our rebellion against God. And the Lord Jesus, as he stood in the synagogue, read Isaiah 61:1, a very similar passage to this: 'The Spirit of the Lord is on me . . . He has sent me to proclaim freedom for the prisoners and recovery of sight for the blind, to set the oppressed free' (Luke 4:18).

And this is how our passage ends:

I am the LORD; that is my name;
  my glory I give to no other,
  nor my praise to carved idols.
Behold, the former things have come to pass,
  and new things I now declare;
before they spring forth
  I tell you of them.
(Verse 8–9, ESV)

Our God – the one true, living and loving God of the universe – deserves the glory from all nations and all people. It is a serious business to steal glory from God. The 'former things' could be what Cyrus, the conqueror, would do in Isaiah 41. The 'new things' could be the things that the Servant will do, as now God speaks in Isaiah 42.

What on earth does this have to do with you and me? I think there are some gospel truths to drive home: the centrality of Jesus, the necessity of Jesus, and the glory and the beauty of Jesus. What do we mean by the centrality of Jesus in our lives, in our churches? Do you know you could walk in and out of church and not speak about Jesus? I don't mean listening to the preacher. I mean you and me talking about the great Lord Jesus. We talk about football, the weather, everything and anything else but the Lord Jesus! We still call ourselves the people of God, the Jesus people who never speak about Jesus! And we have to repent of this. Get used to talking about Jesus! Pray about it on Saturday night, arrive on Sunday morning and say 'Jesus did this for me, from Monday to Saturday'. Would that be a right conversation to have? We get so used to being casual. We talk about anything and everything but Jesus and the cross, salvation, holiness, and the mission of God.

Second, the necessity of Jesus. Do you believe, personally, that you desperately need Jesus to save you from Satan, to forgive you of sin, to grant you new life with God? I do. I've been on the road for quite a while, but I still get messages from my church. I got a message from Andy, a former drug addict. He heard the gospel through our ministry in prison, gave his life to Christ; his life is totally changed. He sent me a message: 'This is the fourth anniversary that I've lived a drug-free life. Pray for me.' Andy is so excited that every day he lives is filled with Jesus and is drug free. And then there was this man whom I will call 'D', and he came from overseas to Singapore for a short holiday, and his parting words to me were, 'The moment I get home, I'll file for divorce because our marriage is so bad.' Over coffee, we opened up the Word of God and I said, 'Every day just talk to Jesus, just speak about Jesus, and see what that does to your marriage.' We Skyped with him and he said, 'Oh Chris, I'm a different man. I'm so different that my three young children said, "Dad is a different man, he didn't get angry today!"' Do you believe that bringing Jesus into any situation will change everything? If I, as a minister of the gospel, a follower of Jesus, no longer believe that, I should give up. Because if Jesus is not Lord of all your moments, he is not Lord at all. Jesus is Lord of that addiction moment, that depression moment, that marriage on the rocks moment. Jesus is Lord of everything.

And so the gospel is Star Wars. Why Star Wars? We are always fighting over who should get the glory, and that leads to so much pain and brokenness in our life. Friends, life without God is full of pain, brokenness and ugliness. The only way to face the ugliness of men and the ugliness of life is to behold the beauty of the Lord Jesus. Someone said to me, 'Unless you know the Lord of the work, you cannot do the work of the Lord.'

Once, in the first few weeks when my son was in his first year of primary school, I was late in picking him up. By the time I arrived in the car park I could see that the teacher had left him. He was standing all by himself, six or seven years old. So I parked the car, ran up to him, got down to his level and said, 'I'm so sorry, Dad was late.' And my son said, 'Don't worry, Dad, I always knew you would come.' 'Behold the Servant of the Lord' is God's way of saying to you and me that no matter how far you are from him, no matter how deep in sin you are, you must always know he will come through for you. And he's come through for us in the giving of Jesus, the Servant of the Lord. To him you turn to find salvation, a new life, and a mission to be sent from Keswick to the ends of the earth.

God's Suffering Servant

Alasdair Paine

Alasdair started as the vicar of The Round Church at St Andrew the Great, Cambridge, in January 2011. He is married to Rachel and they have three children. He became a Christian at university and was a teacher for ten years before being ordained. He has previously served at St Leonard's, Exeter, and Christ Church Westbourne, Bournemouth.

God's Suffering Servant
Isaiah 52:13 – 53:12

Last year I bought a copy of the Tanakh, the Jewish Bible. This consists of the same thirty-nine books we know as the Old Testament, but arranged in a slightly different order. And almost as soon as I'd opened the packet, I couldn't help turning to Isaiah 53. This book is in thousands of synagogues around the world, in many homes of Jewish people, and I thought to myself, 'When this chapter is read, who do people think it is about?'

Do you remember the Ethiopian in the chariot that Philip met in Acts 8? He was asking the same question. He was reading this passage about the Servant of the Lord, who experienced this horrific, disfiguring, mutilating death after an unfair trial. He is condemned to death even though he has done nothing wrong. He offers no resistance at his trial, is numbered with the transgressors and executed with wicked people. He is buried with the rich but, after his death, his days are prolonged and he sees the light of life again. Who is that? Well, with the Gospels in our hand the answer has to be obvious, because the correspondence with the passion of our Lord Jesus Christ is simply amazing. But what is remarkable is that Isaiah himself tells us at the beginning of the book that he received these words from God in the reigns of Uzziah, Jotham, Ahaz and Hezekiah – that is roughly seven centuries before Jesus. To him these events are in the far future, and yet actually he writes of them in the past tense. So certain is God of their fulfilment that it's as if they have already happened even when Isaiah is writing.

This is by far the most quoted Old Testament passage in the New Testament, because it provides such a clear explanation of the death of Jesus and its significance for you and for me. So let's walk through it, starting at chapter 52:13. The heading I'd give for this section is, 'The Puzzle'. It starts with something which seems quite strange. In verse 13, the Lord himself is speaking:

See, my servant will act wisely;
he will be raised and lifted up and highly exalted.

Here is this mysterious figure of the Servant. As you go through Isaiah, the picture is a bit like one of those pictures on *A Question of Sport*, where you've got to spot the mystery sports person, and gradually the pixels get smaller and finer until somebody hits the buzzer and you've got who it is. And as we go through Isaiah this figure is introduced to us in sharper and sharper focus. Earlier on in the book the term 'servant' is used for Israel, but quite clearly it can't mean that here, because Israel is sinful, and here is someone with no sin. This is an individual who is going to be very great, who is going to be 'raised and lifted up and highly exalted.'

But something absolutely terrible is going to happen to him, that is going to disfigure him in such a way that many will be appalled by looking at him (verse 14). He will be a horrific sight, and yet, verse 15 tells us, many, including kings, will 'shut their mouths'. You know when someone very important is banging on about their thing, and there's a moment in the conversation where, even though they're very important and probably quite proud, they begin to realize there is something they don't know and they stop talking and listen. These kings were amazed when this truth is explained to them. So here is a person who has been brutally mutilated beyond human recognition, and yet he will change the world in this extraordinary way. And the puzzle is this: how can someone who looks like such a 'loser', if I may put it like that, change the world like this? Is it because he is simply a hero, a wonderful example of martyrdom for a good cause? Well you might think that on a first look. But actually Isaiah's explanation takes us much deeper.

And so we come now to the heart of the passage, which is Isaiah's astonishing explanation of the death of the Servant. Chapter 53:1, 'Who has believed our message and to whom has the arm of the LORD been revealed?' You would never have guessed what Isaiah is about to say and many, he knew, would reject it. Indeed, when we see what Isaiah really has to say, in a sense it is so shocking, that we too will be tempted to reject the explanation he gives for the death of the Servant. Isaiah explains the Servant grew up unremarkably. However he changed the world, it wasn't by force of personality (verse 2). In fact,

> He was despised and rejected by mankind,
>   a man of suffering, and familiar with pain.
> Like one from whom people hide their faces
>   he was despised, and we held him in low esteem.
> (verse 3)

Isaiah is numbering himself against those who first saw him as a loser or a bad man, and then had their minds changed. Then comes the explanation of why it was that this Servant suffered in the way that he did. He suffered for a purpose. Our first thought was that he must have done something wrong to end up on the wrong side of God. But no, it was for us that he suffered. In verse 5, do you see the 'he' and 'us' language there?

> But he was pierced for our transgressions,
>   he was crushed for our iniquities;
> the punishment that brought us peace was on him,
>   and by his wounds we are healed.

It's as if there has been a great exchange, and somehow he has suffered for us. Isaiah explains he was pierced for our transgressions where we overstepped God's law, he was crushed for our iniquities, our whole sinful mindset. 'The punishment that brought us peace' – that is, forgiveness, peace with God – 'was on *him*, and by his wounds we are healed'. And then in verse 6 we come to the very heart of the passage. 'We all, like sheep, have gone astray.' It's not a particularly complimentary picture of human behaviour. We've got lots of opportunity while we're in Keswick to see sheep and see the clueless way in which they behave. You might know how Handel set this to music in *Messiah*. It's rather jolly music as they sing – 'we all like sheep have gone astray'. The music bounces along as if we find sin pleasurable and happy, and we don't know what a hash we're making of life. And then suddenly the music tone changes: 'and the LORD has laid on him the iniquity of us all'. The change of tone reflects the unspeakable cost and the astonishing, shocking truth of what is asserted in this verse, which is that Jesus took the punishment we deserved for our sin. Our sin was laid on the sinless Son of God.

The Bible tells us that we are under wrath, the holy anger of God, on account of our sin. We're each facing death and hell, and here is Jesus, the one perfect man, and the Lord has laid on him the iniquity of us all. Now I am free. Jesus has taken the burden, willingly. Martin Luther put it this way:

> Our most merciful Father . . . sent his only Son into the world and laid on him all the sins of everyone, telling him to be Peter the denier, Paul the persecutor and blasphemer

and oppressor, to be David the adulterer, to be the sinner
that ate the fruit in Paradise, the thief who hung on the
cross – in short, to be the person who has committed
the sins of everyone.[1]

That is the awesome truth of Isaiah 53:6: 'the LORD has laid
on him the iniquity of us all.' And the word for this transfer
is 'substitution'. If you're a football fan, you're used to
the idea of substitution – one player goes off, another player
goes on. In Isaiah's case it is a substitution of punishment.
I deserve the punishment from God for the way that I've
lived. But Jesus, wonderfully, lovingly, willingly absorbs
that punishment instead. Sometimes that doctrine is called
'penal substitution'. The word 'penal' is related to the word
'penalty', meaning to do with punishment.

And Isaiah won't let us off the hook. He wants to make
sure that we've absolutely got that clear. It's there all
through the passage as he tells the details in advance of the
story of the execution of Jesus:

> He was oppressed and afflicted,
>   yet he did not open his mouth;
> he was led like a lamb to the slaughter,
>   and as a sheep before its shearers is silent,
>   so he did not open his mouth.
> (verse 7)

The thing that mystified Pontius Pilate, as he placed Jesus
on trial, was that Jesus didn't offer a defence. He offers no

defence because of course he goes to the cross willingly. It is in the plan of God. From early on in the Gospels, Jesus is telling his disciples how he must go to Jerusalem and die. There was a shocker of a book a few years ago which compared a Christian understanding of what Jesus did on the cross to 'cosmic child abuse',[2] as if God was doing something horrible to his Son against his will. But the Lord Jesus did it willingly for us. That's why he offered no defence.

People sometimes speak as if the main purpose that God had in giving his Son to die was to show that his Son understands our sufferings. That is a wonderful truth that comes from the death of the Lord Jesus, but that is not the *main* point of the cross. If it had been the main point of the cross why not have Jesus die in a famine, a natural disaster, some act of war, or as a refugee? Instead, he dies in a process of judicial execution – to demonstrate that something judicial is going on here. Sin is being punished (verse 8). Yes, humanly speaking there is a travesty of justice happening at this trial, but in another and more glorious level God is working out his process to sentence human sin and have the Lord Jesus executed as the sentence is passed.

And, verse 9, it's because Jesus was innocent that he was able to take your and my place. He was able to stand in for you and for me and, in fact, he was perfectly qualified in every way. As God the Son, he was God himself, the judge taking the penalty on himself in an extraordinary way. As a human being he was able to take your and my place, and as a sinless human being he had no sin of his own to die for. This is no miscarriage of justice; look at verse 10, 'the LORD makes his life an offering for sin'. That's the language of the ancient guilt-offerings in the book of Leviticus. Jesus is that offering, and this is how the whole New Testament understands Jesus' death. We wouldn't have enough time this evening to look at all the references which make this point. Peter writes, 'He himself bore our sins in his body on the tree.' Being hanged on a tree was a symbol of being under God's curse, 'that we might die to sin and live to righteousness. By his wounds you have been healed' (1 Peter 2:24, ESV). Paul startlingly says in 2 Corinthians 5:21, 'God made him who had no sin to be sin for us, so that in him we might become the righteousness of God.'

And then all through the Gospel accounts, the writers aren't simply telling us the story, they're telling us the meaning of the story. The very evening before he dies there is the Lord's Supper where Jesus explains the significance of his 'blood of the new covenant'. And then the events unfold. The mockers crying, 'He saved others but he can't save himself!' Of course he couldn't. He saved us, that's why he couldn't save himself. Why do you think the Gospel writers tell us about the criminal Barabbas who was set free on that day? Is it not because, as Barabbas walked free that Friday afternoon, and he saw that figure on the cross in the distance, he thought to himself, 'That could have been me.' The crowd were allowed to have one person released. If they had released Jesus, it would be Barabbas on that cross. When you get to John's Gospel, he stresses again and again the connection with the Passover, the

Lamb of God, the lamb that died and whose blood was daubed on the door so that God would pass over that house in Ancient Egypt. The lamb dies so the firstborn son does not need to die. The Gospel writers won't let us leave this alone – Jesus died in our place, as our substitute.

If you're trying to put yourself right with God by what you do, if you're trusting in yourself or your own religion, you will find this idea of Jesus dying in your stead either incomprehensible, unnecessary or offensive. My friends, if you've come by God's grace to understanding that you are a sinner urgently in need of forgiveness, then far from being offensive, this is the most wonderful news in the world! That God should take our sin and lay it on the sacred head of Jesus. Where I live in Cambridge, there was a famous preacher in the late eighteenth century called Charles Simeon. When he arrived as an undergraduate he was shocked to be invited to a service of the Lord's Supper. He had led an absolutely corrupt life at school, and he thought, 'I'm no more fit to turn up at the Lord's Supper than the devil himself.' So while lots of other students were having fun, enjoying the beginning of the new term, Simeon actually started a journey of trying to work out how he could possibly be right with God. Nobody could tell him and, eventually, through reading a book which explained the book of Leviticus, he learnt how the high priest would lay his hands on the sacrificial animal and confess the people's sins. And that to Simeon was the answer. He came to see that that's what the Lord Jesus had done, and on Easter Day he woke up a new man, and a new creation. And thus began a great ministry of wanting to tell other people this news as well.

This point that Jesus died in our place really matters, because of how Isaiah finishes with a description of the life-giving results for us. Verse 10, 'he will see his offspring'. His saving death will lead to many people becoming offspring. One commentator explained that we strayed as sheep and we return as sons. We have the privilege of belonging to this great worldwide family, which is Christ's achievement. Look around you this evening. You are seeing just a small outpost of the vast, countless multitude that this Suffering Servant has bought by hanging and dying on the cross. 'By his knowledge my righteous servant will justify many' (verse 11). Justify – just as if I'd never sinned, or even better, just as if I had lived like the Lord Jesus himself. There is full forgiveness in the blood he shed.

There was once a friend who made it his business to pay for Rachel and me to go out on our wedding anniversary to a very nice restaurant each year. It was an amazing thing because he used to say, 'Just have anything you like!' So we would turn up at this place and go right through the menu and have a tremendous evening. And at the end, we'd never see the bill because another had paid for it. There was nothing for us to pay. There is nothing to pay if we're in Christ. He has paid our debts in full, and all the benefits of the gospel flow from that – adoption as his children and glory in the future. Why? Well, because, verse 11, 'he will bear their iniquities'. That's the word that was used of the scapegoat that was sent out in the desert. After the priest had laid his hands on the goat and confessed the sins of the people, in the days of the Old Testament, the goat would go far away out into the desert to die, as if to symbolize their sins had gone far away. How marvellous to know that the Lord Jesus has dealt with all our sin.

Here is the answer to the puzzle we posed earlier. Why is this apparent loser so great?

> Therefore I will give him a portion among the great,
>> and he will divide the spoils with the strong,
> because he poured out his life unto death,
>> and was numbered with the transgressors.
> For he bore the sin of many,
>> And made intercession for the transgressors.
> (verse 12)

God is so thrilled, if I may put it like this, with the wonderful result of the Saviour's death, who is numbered with the transgressors and made intercession for them and bore their sin, so that God could then adopt a worldwide family as his own. And you know what? Right at the start of the passage it says 'my servant will act wisely; he will be raised and lifted up and highly exalted', and at first glance that simply looks like he will receive all glory. But in John's Gospel, the moment of Jesus being raised up is the moment of the cross; the central glory of the Lord Jesus is his saving death. I'll never forget when I first understood this. I'm no king, but I did shut my mouth because of him. And don't we long for others to hear this? Ponder his love – the one who died in your place and mine, that we might be fully and freely forgiven.

Notes

1. Martin Luther, *Galatians*, The Crossway Classic Commentaries, eds Alister McGrath and J. I. Packer (IVP, 1998), p. 129.
2. Steve Chalke, *The Lost Message of Jesus* (Zondervan, 2004), p. 182.

Contesting

Rodgers Atwebembeire

Rodgers Atwebembeire is the Pastor of New City Community Church, a reformed Presbyterian Church in Uganda's capital, Kampala. He is also the Regional Director for East Africa of the Africa Centre for Apologetics Research, a non-profit, non-denominational charity equipping believers in Africa for the defence and proclamation of the gospel.

Contesting
Acts 17:16–34

Tonight we would like to look at Acts 17. But before we do so, allow me to remind you of a number of things that are critically important. Number one: the Keswick Convention is really about missions. The Keswick Convention is about responding to the mandate of the Great Commission where Jesus calls his disciples and sends them out into the nations of the world to make disciples. It is important that we understand that the Great Commission presupposes a certain context. And some of the things that characterize the context of the Great Commission include the challenge to nations, religious cultures and the world views of the day. In Matthew 28 Jesus sends his disciples to nations, but at that time there were actually no nations. So basically Jesus is sending them across cultures, into the traditions and practices of the people of the time. On

Pentecost day, when he gives them the power to go out, we see the context of the mission field represented by the different people gathered in Jerusalem, speaking different languages, from different countries. Clearly it is a call that is multicultural.

Number two: the Great Commission is a call into a multi-religious context. When Jesus calls his disciples to go out, he is not sending them out because there are no religions. They are not going out to speak to empty minds. They are talking to people who already believe something. In his day the Greeks had their pantheon of gods. The Romans had their shrines, some of them even including idol worship. So when Jesus says, 'Go and make disciples of all nations', he is aware that there are alternative religious spiritualities that vie for competition and prominence, and yet he sends the disciples out to establish the Christian faith.

Why is this important? Because every day, Jesus is sending you and me into a world that basically looks like that of the disciples. We speak to people that already have religious beliefs, except these beliefs are not Christian and quite often they stand in opposition to the Christian world view. And this is exactly what we are looking at tonight. In Acts 17, Paul providentially finds himself in the city of Athens as he waits for his co-workers, Timothy and Silas. As he is moving around the city, looking at their different way of life, their behaviour, their culture, he is distressed by the idolatry that pervades the city. And, as was his custom, he begins to go from synagogue to synagogue proclaiming the Word of God, against the conflicting beliefs, behaviours and world views of that day.

Along the way he is confronted by philosophers, the Stoics and Epicureans, who not only oppose what he preaches but providentially, without intending it, provide an opportunity to give reasons for the hope that is in him. They bring him to the Areopagus and level some accusations against him. 'You preach things that we do not understand. You look like you are a proclaimer of foreign divinities. Can you please tell us who you are and why you believe what you believe? Why are you different from the other Athenians that we have around us? Why do you believe a man called Jesus, whom we have not heard about before?' And you will notice that the questions being posed to Paul are not really new questions. They are questions that we are being bombarded with every day in our workplaces and our families. Our very own children will ask us to make a case for our faith! Wherever we go, people are looking at our behaviour and lifestyle and they wonder why we are different. They wonder why we go to church when we could be going camping, swimming, or touring – they do not understand! And they ask, 'Can you tell us why you are Christian? Why is it that even when you know we believe other things, you continue to want to tell us about your Christianity? Are you saying that everything we believed until you came was wrong? Is that how arrogant your Christianity really is?' People will challenge you and question your world view. They will test it by provoking you to see how you respond. They will talk, watch how you behave, and see if what you believe can stand the challenge of that day.

Are you prepared to give an answer? Can you share your reasons for the hope that is within you? Or do you refer them to your pastor, your church, or to a book you recently read? Or maybe you dodge their questions because you were not prepared to engage? Tonight we want to see how Paul models for us evangelism to people of different religious groups, or to people of competing world views. When confronted by these philosophers, and when given an opportunity to share the hope within him, we see Paul confidently present a gospel that cannot be denied or ignored. In his presentation he will challenge their assumptions, consider their questions, correct their misconceptions, confront their world views, cut down their defences, and compare and contrast the biblical world view with the pre-existing world views that these people held. But even more importantly, he will communicate the gospel in a convincing and compelling manner so that there is no neutral ground when he is done. Either you are in or you are out. He will clarify his Christian beliefs and convictions such that there is no room for misunderstanding. I believe that this is the challenge that you and I have today. We have been called not just to say we are Christian, but to provide reasons as to why we believe what we believe in a convincing and compelling manner. As Christians we must not only stand for the truthfulness and the credibility of our faith, but we must leave people without excuse when we communicate what it is that we believe.

So Paul communicates in a manner that everyone is left without excuse. Paul will actually challenge their assumptions and show them that the God whom they long to know is knowable. He introduced to them a God who is transcendent, operating outside and above creation, but also immanent. As mighty as he is, as sovereign as he is, God has committed himself in relationship with his creation. The Christian faith is the only religion where you meet a God that is personal and relational. You don't just find a God who is high and sovereign, but a God who calls men and women into relationship with him, a God who, instead of seeking to be known as the king, would rather be the father. Paul will remind them that he is not just a God who has created and walked away, but he providentially controls reality. Not only has he created the heavens and the earth at a moment in time, but he is daily and continually involved in his creation. He determines when people are born, how long they live, and when they will die. He is a God who is in charge – and one day he will bring the whole of creation to account, and everyone will have to stand before him to give account.

If God is transcendent and immanent, sovereign and providential, personal and relational, how does humanity compare with him? What are implications of understanding the nature of people and also the relationship that humans should have with this God? Paul reminds them that humankind is fragile and finite. God is not like idols of silver and gold that need to be provided for, given housing and catered for. On the contrary, it is human beings who must continue to depend on God. It is human-kind who has come from God, and not the reverse. It is people who must continue to seek for God, even though God is very near. Paul is essentially saying there is no greater pursuit for any human being than the pursuit of God. You could pursue gold, silver, material things, love, prosperity and success, but in the face of God, in light of eternity, all these things have an expiry date. When all things are said and done, humanity must stand before God. He reminds them that God has not only set a day by which he will judge the world, but sent the man through whom he will judge the world. He has shown this man to the world by raising him from the dead. Paul begins his sermon with creation and general providence, and ends with redemption through the person of Jesus Christ, through whom salvation and the hope of eternal life must be found.

There are a number of principles that we can glean from what Paul is saying that can model for us how we can conduct evangelism to people of different religious and world views. The first principle is **concern**. When we come to Acts 17, we see that Paul is driven to preaching by a concern. He looks at the idols and is very distressed at the wickedness and godlessness that pervades this city. His heart is broken with compassion for the lost. He sees men who look wise, but who are foolish; he sees philosophers who think they know, but actually they are more lost than anyone else. He looks at them and his heart breaks, and he feels he must do something about it. He is like Jesus, who looked at the city of Jerusalem and said, 'Jerusalem, Jerusalem . . . how often I have longed to gather [you] . . . as a hen gathers her chicks under her wings, and you were not willing' (Matthew 23:37). It is out of his broken and compassionate heart that Jesus reaches out, and Paul is doing the same here.

In Matthew 9, as Jesus travelled through the cities and villages healing the sick and preaching, he looked at the crowds. They were tired and weary, 'like sheep without a shepherd', and he had compassion on them (verse 36). And what does he conclude? He says, 'The harvest is plentiful but the workers are few. Ask the Lord of the harvest, therefore, to send out workers into his harvest field' (verses 37–38). Jesus sees a weary and harassed people, and concludes, 'We need more harvesters, more labourers'. He connects the preaching of the gospel to the harassed state of the people. He sees evangelism and gospel proclamation as the antidote to whatever problems and challenges they were going through. Paul looks at the big city in the same way, and he cannot imagine doing anything else than proclaiming the gospel to these people who were harassed by ignorance, sin and idolatry.

Paul does not just have a compassionate heart for the lost, but he has a righteous anger against evil and wickedness, and that is why he has been provoked to say something. What is it that drives your evangelism and discipleship? If it isn't compassion, you won't go far. If you are driven by money from supporters, what happens when supporters stop giving? If you are driven by the opportunity to go to a country outside your own, what happens when that country is invaded by terrorists? What keeps you on the mission field when everything falls apart? Paul would be beaten, persecuted and ridiculed, but he would not quit. He would keep going because seeing the lost broke his heart.

The next C: we need to be aware that when we go out to engage with people, we will find ourselves in what I call a **conflict of world views**. Remember, the people we are speaking to are not empty heads. They already believe things, except that those things are in opposition to the Christian faith. Paul engages the philosophers of that day who had their own theologies that conflicted with the Christian world view. You must be ready to engage with people who will not agree with you, who will not understand what you are talking about, because the culture and the world views from which they come are in contradiction to what Christianity stands for. Many times when we go out to preach, we assume that people have an idea of what we are talking about. But when these philosophers, as smart as they are, listen to Paul, what was their conclusion? 'He's a babbler. He does not know what he's talking about. He's speaking some strange things that probably should not concern us.' If Paul is going to make sense, he must come down to their level, understand where they are coming from, and be able to engage them in a language they understand, using examples and illustrations they acknowledge and appreciate. So Paul will reuse examples from within their own culture. He will appeal to their poets and their philosophers because that is the language they understand. This is the third C – **contextualization**.

So, Paul is driven by concern, encounters conflict of world views, and contextualizes the gospel message. He also makes **connections** with the people he is talking to, he establishes common ground. When he begins to speak, the first thing he does is give them some kind of compliment:

> People of Athens! I see that in every way you are very religious. For as I walked around . . . I even found an altar with this inscription: TO AN UNKNOWN GOD.
> (verses 22–23)

Now Paul had several options that he could have used in his introduction. He could have introduced himself as an apostle, a man with great authority from Jesus, the Son of God. He could have rebuked them for their idolatry and threatened them with the hellfire that awaited them. And you know what? He would have been right. All that would have been true. But how many minutes do you think he would have lasted? By saying they are religious, Paul is not agreeing with their theologies or their religious positions, but complimenting them and acknowledging their personal efforts to strive to find God. He is connecting with them. He is scratching where they itch, so they will listen, they will follow, because he's talking about a subject that is dear to their heart. He connects with them where they are so that he can take them where they need to be: 'You are ignorant of the very thing you worship – and this is what I am going to proclaim to you' (verse 23). Connecting with people is very important if you are going to communicate the gospel to them.

Another 'C': it is important that as we share the gospel, no matter where we begin, we **conclude** with Jesus. We may begin from natural revelation, creation, marriage, funerals or food. But the gospel is not complete unless Jesus is the centre and the consummation of everything we are saying. Today we live in a society that cares more about tolerance than the truth. We live in a society where people would rather be united in lies than divided in error. People are willing to be generic in their communication of the gospel, and therefore essentially vague. They are happy to share about an abstract God who could take the form of anything – a cow in India or ancestors in Africa. But they are afraid to mention the man, Jesus, because then you are talking about the historical Jesus, the man who called himself the Son of God. The man who preached and proclaimed the gospel with authority, who performed miracles and wonders, who died and rose again. You are talking about the man who demands worship and allegiance from everybody, and that causes conflict. Many Christians are willing to talk about their God of love who cares for the poor, so they preach a social gospel where everybody is united, disregarding the Jesus who died on Calvary's cross. But any message, any communication, that does not make Jesus the centre, ultimately is not the gospel.

RODGERS ATWEBEMBEIRE

Paul understands this. He may not begin with Jesus because they have not yet come to a level where they can understand and relate to him, but he brings everything he's talking about to find its consummation in the man, Jesus Christ. He emphasizes at least two important aspects – that this Jesus is the one who died and rose again, and that this Jesus will judge the nations of the world. You can receive him today as the Saviour, or you can wait and meet him face to face as the Judge of the world. So what are you going to do with this Jesus of Nazareth? He's a man you cannot ignore. And ultimately every gospel communication must seek to bring people to that place where they can face Jesus, where they can know Jesus for who he is, and make a decision for or against him. He is the only entrance into eternity (John 14:6). Peter, in Acts 4:12, will say, 'Salvation is found in no one else, for there is no other name under heaven given to mankind by which we must be saved.' Paul understands that it is important to talk about God: his sustaining, providential power and transcendence. But he also knows that the story is not complete until Jesus is the centre of that story. He draws them to Jesus, reminding them that he will judge the nations of the world and they must respond to him at some point in their life, otherwise judgment awaits them.

Finally, we must preach with the aim of **convincing for conversion**. We are not providing information or personal opinions. The goal of our message is to convince people that they really need a relationship with Jesus, that Christianity is unique, supreme, credible, truthful, trustworthy and it is *the only* faith, apart from which humans will perish. Paul understood that, and he preached convincingly. He preached with the goal of conversion, and when he was done with his sermon there were three responses: rejection of what he said, reluctance to make a decision, and the reception from some who believed and followed Jesus. Good evangelism, good gospel communication, aims at convincing men and women, persuading them of the truthfulness, the credibility of the Christian faith against every other world view that they hold. When all is said and done, every knee must bow, every tongue must confess Jesus Christ is Lord, to the glory of God the Father. Praise the Lord.

Gospel Contentment

Jonty Allcock

Jonty is the pastor of The Globe Church in London, which was planted in September 2015. He is married to Linda and they have three boys. After studying chemistry at university, he served at a church in Enfield for fourteen years before moving to central London. He is passionate about people meeting Jesus through the pages of the Bible and then seeing them trained, equipped and sent out for a lifetime of serving Jesus.

Gospel Contentment
Philippians 4:4–23

What a joy to be able to share God's Word with you on this final evening of Keswick. I wonder how you're feeling as you head home. Can I suggest that there's a danger that we go home from Keswick with a sort of Disney view of everything we've heard this week? What I mean is, we've heard loads of things, we've been challenged and inspired. We've heard about God's unstoppable plan, that the gospel will spread, and we've been called to play a part in it. We can go home, saying 'Yes I can!' And I just want to caution us tonight, as we go home, to be careful where our confidence is placed. You see, we are constantly being told that we can do whatever we want to do. Our children know this full well. If I speak to anyone under of the age of about twenty and say, 'Can we fix it?' They say, 'Yes we can!' Of course we can! Bob the Builder tells us! This is Bob the Builder theology.

Our kids are being taught over and over again in school that you can do anything you want, you just have to believe in yourself. Most kids want to be Premier League footballers. They're not going to make it. And on the day they fail, whose fault is it? Well, it's your fault, because you can do anything if you believe in yourself. Just after Geraint Thomas won the Tour de France in 2018, he basically said: 'Kids, just dream big. If people tell you it can't be done, keep going and believe in yourself. With hard work, everything pays off in the end.' That's fine if you've just won the Tour de France, but what about the thousands of other kids who've failed? We're not preparing our kids to fail. We're not preparing them for the real world. We're giving them an expectation and a hope that says, 'It's all about you. Have confidence in yourself.' Paul does not want to send you home with your confidence in you. He's not saying, 'You can do anything, you can change the world, you can convert your friends, if you just *believe* in yourself.' That's not Paul's message. But neither is his message that you're rubbish and you can do nothing.

Paul has a secret for you, did you notice it? The secret comes in verse 13: 'I can do all this through him who gives me strength.' 'Paul, can you do it?' 'Yes I can!' 'How, Paul?' 'Well, because Christ Jesus will give me strength.' So, young people and old people, I want you to dream big dreams. I want you to have bigger ambitions than simply winning a cycling race. I want you to have massive ambitions because it's not you who does it. The world's message is, 'believe in yourself', but the problem is I'm limited. I have limited power, limited wisdom, limited time. I'm severely limited and therefore there's going to be stress, anxiety, discontent when I end up just being mediocre. How do you cope with being mediocre if you've been told all your life that you just need to believe and you can be anything you want? If we keep telling our kids 'you're special' – special means you're entitled to something more than everybody else – no wonder they are growing up so disappointed. This lie about believing in yourself is destroying people.

The resources in you are limited but the resources in Christ are not. Look at verse 19: 'My God will meet all your needs according to the riches of his glory in Christ Jesus.' God has put all of his glorious riches in Christ and he's put the riches of everything in Christ to meet your needs. This is the God who, with a word, spoke creation into being. My words are so weak, but God's words have unlimited power. All of that power, placed in Christ, to meet your needs. This is the God who brought his people out of slavery in Egypt, parted the Red Sea, and defeated the entire Egyptian army. He's put all of that saving power in Christ who died for you. He's put all wisdom in Christ, he's put all strength in Christ, he's put all wealth in Christ. It's all in Christ! Why would you believe in yourself? Paul wants us to go home from Keswick with big ambitions, not believing in ourselves but believing in Christ, where all treasure is found. We're going to work through the passage now and see what it will look like to have your confidence in Christ.

First, *pursue joy with all your heart*. If God has placed all his riches in Christ then 'Rejoice in the Lord always. I will say it again: rejoice!' (verse 4). How do you feel about being commanded to be joyful? You know what it's like: you're in a bad mood and someone comes along and says, 'Cheer up!' You just want to punch them! But Paul is not saying, 'Cheer up'. He is saying, 'See what you have in Christ.' You can't make yourself feel joyful because it's not in you – you won't find joy in you. You don't become joyful by believing in yourself, you get joyful by going to the one in whom God has put all his riches – go to Christ! If you don't feel joyful – when you're standing in church and have no desire to sing, or if you've got to the end of Keswick and everyone around you seems to have had a great time but you feel miserable – may I make a really practical suggestion? Don't pretend, don't fake it. Say to God, 'Heavenly Father, I do not want to worship you, I do not feel joyful.' Just be honest. Then say, 'I'm sorry. I'm sorry because you are always worthy of joy. All the riches of glory are in Christ – how could I not want to worship you?' And then you say, 'Heavenly Father, please give me joy! Make me joyful!' Joy is a fruit of the Spirit, it's a gift from God; you don't believe in yourself, you believe in Christ! You say, 'I don't feel joyful. I'm sorry, please give me joy.' And then you open your mouth and start to sing. And you sing defiantly, defiant in the face of your misery. I am going to be joyful, because Christ is worthy of my joy. And maybe, just maybe, the feelings might follow. But don't settle for joylessness. Believing in Christ means you will pursue joy. Sing your heart out. The times when you should sing loudest are the times when your heart feels coldest, right? Don't let the coldness of your heart dictate how loud you sing. I think you need to ask Christ to change your heart, and pursue it.

Here's the second application: *display gentleness*. Verse 5, 'Let your gentleness be evident to all.' If life is all about achieving my dreams, goals and ambitions, then I will be brutal towards others, because they'll get in my way. So here I am, in the music group, playing the bassoon because that's my spiritual gift. I think I'm pretty good. Then in walks one of the world's greatest bassoonists who says, 'I'd like to join your church.' Oh, she's going to get in my way. I will snap her reed! You see, gentleness comes from knowing that it's not all about you. Gentleness comes from knowing that God has put all riches in Christ. Praise the Lord that there's someone better than me at the bassoon! People don't have to listen to me any more! Gentleness is about letting go of my rights; gentleness is about saying it's not all about me. I can let it go. Jesus gave up all of his rights. Gentleness isn't about weakness. Jesus wasn't weak. Jesus was phenomenally strong and he gave it up for you.

Can I suggest a couple of things? Some of you will be driving home tomorrow. Why don't you practise a bit of gentleness in your driving? Why don't we practise in our families when there are different-sized portions of apple crumble? Display gentleness and do it because if you don't practise there, if you don't display it there, you're never going to do it in the big things. Brothers and sisters, if all of the riches of God lie in Christ, you can let go of everything. You can get your apple crumble and go, 'Let me give you a bit more. There you go, have more! Because I've got Christ, it's all I need!' Why display gentleness? Because, 'The Lord is near.' Do you see how Paul has got the Lord always in his view? It could mean that the Lord is near in the sense of close. I think it's more likely to mean that his coming is near. And man, when you have to face Jesus and he says, 'Why did you fight about that apple crumble?' that's going to be a hard one to answer.

Number three: *fight anxiety*. Our culture is so stressed. Why? Because you've got to achieve your dream. You've got to do brilliantly in your exams because if you don't then your whole life's rubbish. No wonder we're stressed! Anxiety happens when the resources that I have don't match the situation that I face. So if I'm facing something I know I don't have the strength, money or time for, I begin to stress about it. Anxiety is a symptom of self-reliance. Let me say something, and I want to be absolutely serious and clear about this. To feel anxious is not a sin. What you do with your anxiety is the key. You see, there is a sort of anxiety that will drive you to yourself and to running around like a headless chicken – at that point, because you are putting your confidence in yourself, that is sin. But if your anxiety drives you somewhere else, that is glorious. Every time you feel anxious is an opportunity to run to Christ, in whom is hidden all the treasures of wisdom and knowledge, in whom all the glorious riches of God dwell.

God doesn't say, 'Do not be anxious – right, next.' He says, 'Don't be anxious . . . but in every situation, by prayer and petition, with thanksgiving, present your requests to God' (verse 6). It's exactly what he's been saying all the way through this chapter. Get your confidence in God, the one who loves you and gave his Son for you. Trust him. Bring your requests to him and come with thanksgiving, remembering the blessings he has given you.

Is a family, work or health situation really stressing you out? Tonight, God says, 'Don't be anxious. Run to me. I have the resources for you. It's not going to be easy, but I will go with you through it.' And as we experience that, God's peace – which transcends understanding – guards our hearts and our minds. As soon as an anxious thought comes into your head, as soon as you begin to worry, say, 'This is an opportunity for me to rely on Christ!'

Number four: *aim higher*. Look at verse 8: 'Finally, brothers and sisters, whatever is true, whatever is noble, whatever is right, whatever is pure, whatever is lovely, whatever is admirable – if anything is excellent or praiseworthy – think about such things.' We can be so careless with our thought life. Social media fills our heads with videos of kittens and donkeys that can play the violin, and we watch them for hours. It's complete junk! We're filling our heads with rubbish rather than with what is true and noble. What you think about feeds your mind and shapes you as a person. And tonight, if we're going to set all of our hope in Christ, it will mean aiming higher in our thinking. Think about what is true, noble, right, pure, lovely, admirable, excellent and praiseworthy. We could certainly start with Christ, the most lovely of all men, the most excellent and admirable, the most praiseworthy. Imagine if you spent a fraction of the time that you spend watching videos or telly thinking of Christ, enjoying Christ, reading of Christ, knowing him more. Think what a difference it would make to you.

You may say, 'I can't get in control of my thinking, I can't change.' You're right, you can't. But Christ can. And so here we are again saying, 'Jesus, please, help me to aim higher. Help me to set aside my mind for things that are good.' You know, I think we've lost the discipline of fasting. I don't just mean fasting from food, but fasting from other stuff in order that we might give ourselves to contemplate the worth of Jesus. When was the last time you deliberately gave something up so you could spend time thinking of Jesus? If you're into social media, why not give up social media for a week? Spend that time aiming higher, thinking of Christ.

Fifth, *learn contentment* (verse 10). Here Paul gets to the point of why he's writing this letter. He's writing to say thank you to them for the gifts that they've sent him. But he wants them to know that his circumstances don't define his contentment. He has learned the secret of contentment, and that is that he's transferred his contentment from stuff to Jesus. We have this relentless desire for more, don't we? I love getting new stuff. I was so excited about getting a new mobile phone. And for a little while I'm like, 'Look at this, it's new! It's my iPhone 3!' And then there's an advert for the iPhone 10. Arrgh, now I've got to wait two years until I can get one of those! This is how we are all the time, because we tie our contentment to our stuff. If you tie your contentment to what you get, you are doomed to a life of disappointment and frustration because it will never, ever satisfy you. But Paul says, 'I've learnt the secret of contentment. I don't care whether I've got lots of stuff or no stuff because I've got Christ' – and that sets you free to enjoy life. Do you notice that Paul didn't say that he always has nothing? Paul says, 'I know what it is to be satisfied when I've got a lot.' I think it's hard to be satisfied when you've got a lot because you want more. And so Paul says, 'Actually what I have experienced is that whether I've got a lot or whether I've got nothing, Christ is everything.' Perhaps tonight you are deeply discontented with your life and tonight God is saying to you, 'My precious child, I want you to learn contentment. I want you to learn what you have in Christ. I want you to delight in it. Go home from Keswick more content than when you arrived.'

And finally, Paul encourages us to *embrace neediness*. Paul was in need and the church in Philippi sent him money. If Disney is right, and if life is all about pursuing your own dreams, you will never admit you are in need because that's weak. You need to sort yourself out; you need to achieve your own goals. We live in a culture where if someone is described as 'needy' they are a little bit sad, a little bit deficient. But when Jesus died on the cross, Mark 15:41 tells us that there were some women who had followed him from Galilee, who had 'cared for his needs'.

When Christ became a man, he became needy. He needed a mother and a father to care for him when he was a baby. He needed these women to provide for him. And we've got to get over ourselves. Often you hear people say, 'Well, I don't want to be a burden . . .' Why don't you want to be a burden? That's the story of the human life! When my children were born, they were a burden to me! They made my life harder! As they got older they're still a burden. But I think there might be a glorious moment in the middle when we can just be happy together, and then I become a burden to them!

That is the story of what it means to be human. And to claim that you don't want to be a burden, to claim you don't want to be needy, is to deny what it means to be human. You need people and people need you. If you are in need, do not be embarrassed to receive help. Our churches should be places where we are needy and we are a burden to one another. And if you have resources, then look for those in need. That's what the Philippian church was doing. Paul says that their gifts are a beautiful, 'fragrant offering' to God (verse 18). God sees it and he's pleased. Of course, if it all depends on you, you'll keep all your money to yourself because it's yours. But if all the resources are in Christ then you just give stuff away, all the time! When was the last time you gave something away? Jesus said to sell what you have and give to the poor. When have you sold something to give to the poor? Because of eBay it's easy to sell stuff. Sell it and give money to the poor – we should do more of this! It's what the Philippians were doing.

We need to finish. All the resources are in Christ and that is why verse 20 is so magnificent: 'To our God and Father be glory for ever and ever. Amen.' If you do anything good as a result of this week, it will be Christ in you – not you – and therefore he will get the glory. So take these six things – I recognize you can't take all of them, maybe one or two that particularly strike you – and say, 'Lord, I want to work on that, please would you help me, give me strength.' Pursue joy, display gentleness, fight anxiety, aim higher, learn contentment and embrace neediness.

Keswick Resources
Enjoy the 2018 Convention!

All the teaching from Keswick 2018 is available, and here are the various options available to you:

1. Free mp3 downloads of Bible readings, evening celebrations and lectures
Please go to the Keswick Ministries website and listen to or download the mp3s. All you need to do is register, and then all downloads are free of charge. Here's the link: https://keswickministries.org/resources/keswick-talk-downloads.

2. Essential Christian
All teaching – Bible readings, evening celebrations, seminars and lectures – is available in various formats, including CD, DVD, mp3 and also USB stick. These can be purchased from Essential Christian. Please go to www.essentialchristian.com/keswick.

Other Keswick teaching is also available from this site, and you can browse the Bible teaching catalogue as far back as 1957! You can also browse albums by worship leaders and artists who have performed at Keswick, including Stuart Townend, Keith and Kristen Getty, plus Keswick Live albums and collections of popular DVDs. To order, visit www.essentialchrisitian.com/keswick or call 0845 607 1672.

3. Free online viewing of Bible readings and lectures

Keswick Convention Bible readings and lectures are also available on Clayton TV at www.clayton.tv. Select what you would like to see, and watch the talks online.

Please encourage others to benefit from these Keswick resources.

Thank you!

KESWICK MINISTRIES

Our purpose
Keswick Ministries is committed to the spiritual renewal
of God's people for his mission in the world.

God's purpose is to bring his blessing to all the nations
of the world. That promise of blessing, which touches
every aspect of human life, is ultimately fulfilled
through the life, death, resurrection, ascension and
future return of Christ. All of the people of God are
called to participate in his missionary purposes,
wherever he may place them. The central vision of
Keswick Ministries is to see the people of God equipped,
encouraged and refreshed to fulfil that calling, directed
and guided by God's Word in the power of his Spirit,
for the glory of his Son.

Our priorities
Keswick Ministries seeks to serve the local church
through:

- *Hearing God's Word*: the Scriptures are the foundation
  for the church's life, growth and mission, and *Keswick
  Ministries* is committed to preach and teach God's
  Word in a way that is faithful to Scripture and relevant
  to Christians of all ages and backgrounds.

- *Becoming like God's Son*: from its earliest days the Keswick movement has encouraged Christians to live godly lives in the power of the Spirit, to grow in Christlikeness and to live under his lordship in every area of life. This is God's will for his people in every culture and generation.
- *Serving God's mission*: the authentic response to God's Word is obedience to his mission, and the inevitable result of Christlikeness is sacrificial service. *Keswick Ministries* seeks to encourage committed discipleship in family life, work and society, and energetic engagement in the cause of world mission.

Our ministry

Keswick: the event. Every summer the town of Keswick hosts a three-week Convention, which attracts some 15,000 Christians from the UK and around the world. The event provides Bible teaching for all ages, vibrant worship, a sense of unity across generations and denominations, and an inspirational call to serve Christ in the world. It caters for children of all ages and has a strong youth and young adult programme. And it all takes place in the beautiful Lake District – a perfect setting for rest, recreation and refreshment.

Keswick: the movement. For 140 years the work of Keswick has had an impact on churches worldwide, and today the movement is underway throughout the UK, as well as in many parts of Europe, Asia, North America, Australia, Africa and the Caribbean. *Keswick Ministries* is committed to strengthening the network in the UK and beyond, through prayer, news, pioneering and cooperative activity.

Keswick resources. *Keswick Ministries* is producing a growing range of books and booklets based on the core foundations of Christian life and mission. It makes Bible teaching available through free access to mp3 downloads, and the sale of DVDs and CDs. It broadcasts online through Clayton TV and annual BBC Radio 4 services. In addition to the summer Convention, *Keswick Ministries* is hoping to develop other teaching and training events in the coming years.

Our unity

The Keswick movement worldwide has adopted a key Pauline statement to describe its gospel inclusivity: 'for you are all one in Christ Jesus' (Galatians 3:28). *Keswick Ministries* works with evangelicals from a wide variety of church backgrounds, on the understanding that they share a commitment to the essential truths of the Christian faith as set out in our statement of belief.

Our contact details

T: 01768 780075
E: info@keswickministries.org
W: www.keswickministries.org
Mail: Keswick Ministries, Rawnsley Centre, Main Street, Keswick, Cumbria CA12 5NP, England

"Let anyone who is thirsty come to me and drink"

JOHN 7:37

CONVENTION 2019

LONGING

WEEK
ONE
13-19 July

🎤 **JOHN RISBRIDGER**

WEEK
TWO
20-26 July

🎤 **VAUGHAN ROBERTS**

WEEK
THREE
27 July - 2 August

🎤 **RAY ORTLUND**

KESWICKMINISTRIES.ORG/CONVENTION

📘 KeswickConvention   📞 017687 80075

🐦 @KeswickC   @ info@keswickministries.org